# THE SEEDS OF GREATNESS ARE WITHIN YOU: A MEMOIR

# THE SEEDS OF GREATNESS ARE WITHIN YOU: A MEMOIR

## WAYNE DAWSON
## WITH DEANTE YOUNG

Dirty Truth Publishing
Cleveland, Ohio
1st Edition

First Edition, November 2022

For information about booking authors Wayne Dawson or Deante Young to speak at your live event, please email Dirty Truth Publishing at dy@deanteyoung.com.

Manufactured in the United States of America

Library of Congress Control Number: 2022917457

ISBN: 978-1-7369466-6-4 (paperback)

978-1-7369466-7-1 (e-book)

Dedicated to my mother, Annie L. Dawson,
my wife LaVerne, my three daughters Tammy, Crystal, and Danielle,
my son Tyshin, my eight grandchildren, and my friend Herb Thomas.

To God be the glory.

# Contents

# Foreword

# By Stefani Schaefer

If you are reading this book, you already know a little bit about Wayne Dawson. Wayne has funneled his passion, expertise, curiosity, and his love for journalism into building a long and distinguished career as a television news reporter and anchor. Born and raised in Cleveland, Ohio, Wayne has treasured the city that has honored him to become Cleveland's most well-loved news anchor.

Wayne is a father of four children and truly cherishes his time with his adorable grandchildren. Wayne puts his heart and soul into serving the people of Cleveland and is dedicated to uplifting our city and all who live here. All of this you probably already knew. What you might not realize is that Wayne and his brother Will (The Honorable Judge William Dawson) have created the Annie L. Dawson Foundation in honor of their dear late mother, Annie. She not only raised two amazing human beings during the most difficult times, but also instilled high morals and values in both of them that live on today.

The Dawson Foundation has donated coats, food, and other critical items to children and families of Cleveland, and they support local students on their journey and pathway to success with yearly college scholarships. They truly uplift!

You also might not know Wayne and his beautiful wife LaVerne have dedicated their lives to being ambassadors of Jesus Christ. Every week, they welcome Clevelanders to worship, pray, and gather to celebrate our Lord and Savior through their ministry at Grace Tabernacle Baptist Church. Wayne truly walks the walk and talks the talk.

Wayne Dawson has the biggest heart of anyone you will ever meet. He has a sympathetic ear and was truly blessed with a gift for making everyone he meets feel as though they have known him for their entire life! Wayne is a friend to ALL. His friendship over the last 30 years is one of the greatest blessings in my life!

He has mastered waking up the people of Northeast Ohio for over two decades—and he loves every minute of it! Every morning on television, when he says, "It is the dawn of yet another beautiful day on the North Coast…" you should know that he is smiling from ear to ear and so thankful you chose HIM to wake you up!

I know you will enjoy this book filled with meaningful stories and treasured relationships. I also know you will find your heart filling with love and deep appreciation for Cleveland's Sharpest and Best Dressed Newsman!

May God Bless You!

Stefani Schaefer,
Wayne Dawson's co-anchor and, more importantly, dear friend

Prologue

# The Moment of Destiny

My life has been full of blessings that could've only come from the King of Kings and the Lord of Lords. How else do you explain a kid, born and raised in the unforgiving streets of Cleveland, earning a life full of miracles that saved him from himself time and time again?

As I reflect on my journey that took me from a childhood filled with extraordinary dreams manifested in a long career in television, community involvement, life-changing relationships as a father and husband, and a sacred commitment to God—I keep trying to pinpoint the single moment that defined my life and purpose.

Many people and experiences shaped me and helped me evolve as a Man of God, but that special occasion on September 16, 2018, brought real context to what God wanted me to do with all He had given me.

This was the day of my ordination to officially become a pastor.

By the time that touchstone Sunday came, I had been at Grace Tabernacle Baptist Church for about a year as their interim pastor, filling in for the late Reverend Dr. Jeremiah Pryce.

I was just preaching God's word while assisting in many decision-making processes in the church.

It felt like an out-of-body experience when I was installed because the church was packed. There were even people in the overflow room to witness what would become the most significant event of my life.

I couldn't help but think, "Wow–this is really happening!"

I looked around and saw so many familiar faces—my wife LaVerne, my children, Reverend Dr. Stephen Rowan, who preached my installation as pastor, Bishop Joey Johnson, Pastor Kevin James, the Reverend Dr. David Hunter and a blur of so many other key figures in my life.

When I got home that night, I thought, "Lord, what have you done?" At first, it was a bit overwhelming knowing God had blessed me with the responsibility of leading His people.

Becoming the pastor of Grace was a privilege that carried with it an enormous responsibility to serve selflessly and deliver God's message to many.

None of that would've been possible if it weren't for the "seeds of greatness" that my Lord and Savior placed in me from Day One. I've seen God use my problems to change me, and He will do that for you if you turn them over to Him.

My favorite Bible verse is Philippians 4:13, "*I can do all things through Christ who strengthens me.*" In these pages, I want you to gain inspiration from my journey and use it with God's will to live your destiny.

# Part I: Deliver Us From Evil

This is the introductory section of Wayne Dawson's historic journey. The title is taken from Matthew 6:13 of the King James Version of the Bible that states:

*"And lead us not into temptation but deliver us from evil: For thine is the kingdom, and the power, and the glory, forever. Amen."*

Because this section covers the key events of Wayne's life from his birth to his early years as a news anchor, there were so many moments in which there were temptations, heartbreak, setbacks, and tragedies in his life as well as those closest to him.

Therefore, a spiritual and God-fearing family such as the Dawsons would likely pray to the Lord to "deliver [them] from evil." Indeed, the enemy knows our weaknesses and there were many to be attacked during the decades covered here.

Please understand that Wayne's constitution and foundation were constructed during this period. You will come to realize that, as the man himself says, "It's not where you start, it's where you're going."

Let's start.

-D.Y.

# Chapter 1

# They Spoke Life Into Me

*Try to be a rainbow in someone else's cloud.*
—Maya Angelou

A proper environment is so important when raising a child, and for me, it became the foundation on which I developed an extreme belief in myself from an early age. Like most of us, I don't remember much from when I was a baby, but I remember the years that followed. That's when my mom, grandparents, aunts, and uncles always spoke life into me. Words of encouragement can go a long way in helping to shape a person's future, and my family made sure my mind was finely tuned for the success that I would eventually have.

I was the first child born to Annie Louise and George William Dawson on April 24, 1955, at Mt. Sinai Hospital. They named me Wayne Doyle Dawson, Doyle after my godfather Lodie "Doyle" Couch who was my father's employer at the time of my birth. For the first decade of my life, we lived in the Glenville area of Cleveland on East 105th Street and Drexel Avenue.

Mom was a hairstylist and a beauty school instructor during those days, after graduating as the valedictorian of her class at Glenville High School, and she was a stickler for education. Something as simple as learning my spelling words was so important to her, and my mom would be in tears until I got those words right. She understood the discipline involved in successful learning. Thinking back, it seems the only times she would become upset with me was because of my schoolwork, because she knew how important it was to my future success.

"Education is the only way that you're going to make it in this life," my mom often told me. She would've been a great mate for a progressive man because she really pushed people to be their best. My dad had a ninth-grade education and was all "personality." He was very intelligent, but coming from the country (Harveysburg, Ohio), his vision for his life was limited.

Although no one in my family was college-educated, they all had decent jobs. My grandparents on both sides always poured positive words of affirmation into me and made me feel that I indeed had the seeds of greatness within me.

"Wayne, where I didn't achieve, you're *going* to achieve," Mom would say. She always told me stuff like that, and the more I heard it from her, the more it started sinking in. So, she and other members of my family laid those seeds of success early on. I remember my Aunt Betty, who was my dad's sister and lived in Cincinnati, would say, "Yeah, Wayne, you're going to be something one day, and I'm going to be your secretary when you grow up," and I'd be like, "Aunt Betty, what are you talking about?"

But the point is that my family would always say stuff like that to me and little did I know, I needed to hear it.

With all that positive reinforcement, it's probably not a coincidence that I dreamed big throughout my childhood. First, I wanted to be a bus driver, then a preacher because I admired my pastor at the time, the Reverend Dr. Albert T. Rowan, who was a great Christian role model. Then I had the audacity to think I could be the president of the United States. Keep in mind that this was the 60s, but I had a youthful imagination and was a fan of John F. Kennedy and the whole "Camelot" thing. Even though we as black people were still fighting to be treated as first class citizens in this country during the Civil Rights Movement, I still believed I was just as good as anyone else. My thinking was, regardless of color, and with hard work, I could achieve my dreams. Once again, I attribute this attitude to the positive affirmations from my family and the fact God had called me to do wonderful things even though at the time, I did not understand that.

Early in my life I was an overachiever. I took pride in being the smartest person in the class during my elementary school years, even going so far as to wonder who my competition was at the beginning of each school year.

During the first half of the 20th century, the Glenville area of Cleveland was a mostly Jewish neighborhood. Many synagogues were built on East 105th Street, but by the 1960s they had become African-American churches.

Bethany Baptist Church was my family's place of worship and it was within walking distance from our Drexel home. Here, Pastor A.T. Rowan's dynamic preaching and teaching helped to influence me to become a believer in Jesus. This was indeed a rich time in my life because my mother's parents (my grandparents) were still alive and since we lived with them on Drexel, it allowed me to spend time with them in and out of church. My grandfather, Armfield Johnson, was a deacon.

Unfortunately, by the time I was eight years old, my grandparents had passed away, and we were forced to sell the family home on Drexel. That caused us to move into an apartment on East 128th Street between St. Clair and Shaw Avenue, which was still in the Glenville area.

I attended several elementary schools during my early years, and one of them, Murray Hill in Little Italy, was racially integrated. This was made possible because of *Brown v. Board of Education,* a landmark decision by the United States Supreme Court in 1954, ruling racial segregation in public schools was unconstitutional. Because of that, I was bussed from Hazeldell Elementary School in Glenville to Murray Hill in Little Italy.

Bussing was the court's way of closing the education gap between blacks and whites. Because black schools were woefully underfunded, the solution was to send black children to all-white schools outside their neighborhoods. Around the country, this became known as the Desegregation Era. At the time, I had no idea how much this decision would influence my life in later years.

My time at Murray Hill was my first real exposure to white people. I remember the Italian kids and their parents throwing rocks at our bus and shouting racial slurs, especially toward the end of the school year.

Ironically, I spent two years as a student at Murray Hill, and the only fight I ever got into was with another black kid. He had been bullying me all year, and we finally got into a fight—something that never happened with the white kids. But this *one* brother! I was like, "What's up with him?"

Despite that nonsense, I continued to apply myself as a student, determined to be the smartest person in class. I would get upset if I got a "B" on an assignment or my report card.

The 1960s were an interesting time in America. The grown-ups were always talking about the turmoil and racism in the country, especially in our city, and it usually didn't bother me.

But that all changed during the months after I completed fifth grade.

The memories of the Hough riots during the summer of 1966 are still vivid, because I was a young kid scared to death as I watched crowds of people burn down our communities. Even then, I could not understand why people would destroy their own neighborhoods, but that's exactly what they did. The negative energy from those situations was a symptom of larger problems plaguing black communities across the nation, including racial discrimination and second-class citizenship, ultimately leading to poverty.

Little did I know, poverty and my own deviant actions were about to become a real problem for my mother.

## Takeaways from Chapter 1

### by Deante Young

To truly understand the extraordinary success that found its way to Wayne Dawson during his lengthy career in broadcasting, you need only to examine his formative years.

Wayne reminds me of a skyscraper because a skyscraper is a wondrous human achievement when observed in its completed form. But the tireless hours, days, weeks, and years that go into its construction are invisible unless you've witnessed it firsthand.

In this chapter, "They Spoke Life Into Me," Wayne allows us to witness the foundational elements that built him into a man who has towered over the city of Cleveland like a skyscraper. He has meant so much to the city, and most of his value and generosity go unnoticed.

Because of his family's consistent infusion of positivity and reassurance, Wayne's mindset was optimized for greatness and calibrated to handle the setbacks and challenges he faced growing up.

Human beings need to believe in themselves if they are ever going to achieve anything. Wayne's unshakable faith in himself, even as a child, is noteworthy considering how easy it is to be dragged down by insecurity and self-doubt.

His mother, Annie Dawson, was the catalyst in cultivating his early self-image, which allowed him to dream of someday becoming a preacher or even the president of the United States. He has undoubtedly transferred that "dreamer's mindset" to many people over the years.

Wayne also had the good fortune of being born at the precise moment in history when harmful restrictions for blacks began to shift. The milestone *Brown v. Board of Education* court ruling made possible the diversity that Wayne experienced throughout school. That helped to shape his sensibilities and make him more aware of the cultural makeup of society.

Bottom line: Even though Wayne Dawson eventually became a college graduate while earning essential degrees, his most important education came at home before he reached his teens. People that care about you will encourage your dreams and ambitions, so it's a great practice to spend time around them.

---

**Wayne Dawson is living proof of that.**

---

# Chapter 2

# Reckless

*I am who I am today because*
*of the choices I made yesterday.*
—Eleanor Roosevelt

Throughout elementary school, I was an exceptional student, and my grades always reflected that. I couldn't have been more blessed in all areas of my life, though I didn't realize it at the time.

I finished sixth grade a couple of months after my twelfth birthday, completely unaware of the big twists and turns my life was about to take. I started middle school for the 1967-68 term, but that wasn't the only transition I was dealing with.

Mom and Dad decided to move us yet again, so we left the apartment on East 128th and ended up in East Cleveland. It was a new beginning, especially because living in East Cleveland was considered an upgrade from the Glenville neighborhood. There was only a difference of a mile or so in proximity, but I was excited, nonetheless.

My academic performance for the first semester of seventh grade was pitch-perfect, with straight A's across the board. I really benefited from the positive teachings of my household in my early years, and it prepared me for any teasing I might endure from my peers.

Whatever kids said to me in middle school paled in comparison to what my family had put into me, so it didn't even matter. I just didn't process the negative things that kids were saying because my self-esteem was so tight that I didn't care. Yeah, I may have felt bad for a few minutes if somebody dogged me out, but it wasn't going to sink in.

Keep in mind I wore thick glasses throughout my life, and was often called "four eyes" and "goggles" by my peers, but I kept it moving anyway because, as I said before, my life was enviable to others in many ways. As an only child, I received all the attention, and self-confidence wasn't an issue. I also had something many kids didn't have: two loving parents who were present.

But as the saying goes, "all that glitters is not gold."

Mom and Dad were very supportive of me, but looking back on those days, the truth is hard to admit. They had a very turbulent marriage that consisted of arguments and sometimes physical abuse on the part of my father.

With no brothers or sisters, I bore the brunt of those encounters, often listening to them argue from the loneliness of my bedroom. On the flip side, they were also excellent role models for me, so it's very interesting how two opposite things can be true at the same time.

Mom and Dad were hard workers, and they modeled what being dedicated to a job, being on time, and doing your best work was all about. From them, I learned the lessons of giving 100% in whatever job I had, whether I was cleaning floors, cutting grass, washing dishes, or delivering newspapers.

I always wanted to do my best, and those early lessons have allowed me to remain at Channel 8 for more than 40 years.

Nonetheless, midway through seventh grade came the arrival of 1968, which would turn out to be a year of crisis for America in general and my household in particular. The arguments between my parents continued to escalate, and I started hanging with the wrong crowd in school.

We then lived on Orinoco Avenue off Hayden Avenue in East Cleveland. I somehow found refuge with the guys at school and around the neighborhood—a break from a home life that was becoming more turbulent and suffocating each day.

As the school year progressed, I started thinking more about girls. In fact, that was a constant source of conversation for us guys, even as I tried my hand at athletics, which led me to be the second-string quarterback on the Kirk Junior High JV football team.

Finally, the negative influences that were growing in my life led me to turn to alcohol and drugs, which is a terrible thing for a 13-year-old kid. Subsequently, my grades suffered, which began a downward spiral of educational underachievement.

Yes, I am a child of the 60s, and the influences of that turbulent time in America had a profound effect on my young life. Despite the fact my interest in education was waning, I became engrossed in the music of the day. From the inspirational lyrics of groups like The Impressions with their 1968 hit song, "We're a Winner," to James Brown's "Say it Loud, I'm Black and I'm Proud," I felt very optimistic. I also gained a sense of self-realization and pride from the works of the Reverend Dr. Martin Luther King Jr., Malcolm X and others. Indeed, the culture of Black Power solidified my blackness and showed me I could do whatever I wanted.

Despite the violence happening in the country with Malcolm X, Dr. King, President John F. Kennedy and Senator Robert Kennedy being killed, along with the shootings and the violence near my own neighborhood, it was a great period because I developed pride in being a young black man.

That time in the world helped to shape my identity.

I'll say it again: I was never the type who felt my color would hold me back; I just never bought into that line of thinking. I praise God for that, and maybe it was because of the little time I spent at Murray Hill, where I achieved excellence alongside white students. I realized that I was just as good as they were, which meant I could do whatever they could.

It's funny how the Lord ordered my steps all along the way because besides college, Murray Hill was the only time I was in school with white students, and the confidence I gained from that experience was important.

Once again, it proved that I could compete with anyone.

The summer of '68 brought the Glenville riots, just two years after Hough, but they hit even closer to home and affected my family a lot more because my father had a store with pinball machines and other games.

His store was on East 117th and Superior, right down the street from where the riots started on Ashbury Avenue. I remember him staying in his store all night with his shotgun, anticipating the rioters breaking in.

By this point, the 1960s had already been a violent era, but it was also a defining era. The Black Power Movement fueled my pride in being black just as much as King and Malcolm X did, and it all strengthened my sense of self.

Any example of achievement and power from a black person only served to expand my inspiration. On the first day of 1968, Carl Stokes officially took office after being elected one of the first black mayors of a major American city. His groundbreaking success showed me that if he could do it, I could do it too.

Although I never saw my race as a limitation to what I could achieve, reality did hit me in the face a few times. When I was in middle school, my family and I drove south to spend time with an aunt who lived in Daytona, Florida. In southern Georgia, not too far from the Florida panhandle, I experienced it firsthand when I saw racially segregated bathrooms for the first time in my life. There was a "colored" bathroom and a "white" bathroom and I thought to myself, "Whoa," because I couldn't believe it.

Yes, I did use the "colored" bathroom.

I had never seen such blatant racism. It stuck with me but didn't deter my dreams, hopes, or goals. I think the nurturing I got as a young person ultimately drove me when I went through my desert experiences because the positive reinforcements I received really sunk in. Whenever I got off track, I knew I could get back on track.

Eighth grade continued the downward slide of my performance in school that began during the second half of seventh grade. My father's presence in the home also became more sporadic.

He and Mom just didn't see eye to eye very often, and it kept getting worse. I turned 14 in the spring of 1969, and as Mom grieved the deteriorating situation with Dad while working a lot more, I felt I had the freedom to do what I wanted.

They say that when you hang around nine fools, you'll soon become the tenth. So, it's not surprising that my grades started falling dramatically once I started hanging out with guys who were so off the chain. All we seemed to care about were girls and drugs.

School work wasn't a top priority; it was all about getting high and chasing girls. As I've said before, my mom was always a big inspiration. Still, she was going through the emotions of losing her marriage which gave me the opportunity to do plenty of crazy things with my life, none of which I am proud of today.

There were times when I would leave for school, and after Mom would go to work, my friends and I would circle back to cut class at my house. I took big-time advantage of the situation when things got rocky between Mom and Dad.

The days of being a straight-A student who loved school were becoming a distant memory. Moving to East Cleveland and hanging out with that particular group created a massive downward spiral into academic mediocrity.

My best friend's sister would say to me, "Wayne, you were an A student until you started hanging out with so-and-so. Look at you now!"

By the time I entered Shaw High School in September 1969, my weed smoking and wine drinking had increased as I tried to blend in with my friends. An older guy in our group provided us with weed, wine, and all the other stuff we tried. It was during this time that the enemy had his hands on me as I routinely drank MD 20/20, Wild Irish Rose, Boone's Farm, and I would also have a mixed drink every now and then. Keep in mind I was only 15 years old.

The older guy was a negative influence, and from the middle of seventh grade to twelfth grade, I barely got by because I was no longer applying myself. I went from being a really good student to being a total slacker who didn't care about anything.

I wanted to get high not only to be accepted by my friends, but I felt that it gave me the confidence I needed to impress the girls. I would do a little schoolwork here and there, but every Friday, we did drugs before school. There was a little diet pill called a Ceco which was a lot like speed back in the day. All week, I'd be in class halfway asleep, not paying attention, but on those Fridays, I'd take the Ceco, and bam, I had everything to say.

This was a dark period in my life, and during my sophomore year at Shaw in 1970-71, I wanted to play football, but I ran track instead. Soon after, Mom found out she was pregnant, and coincidentally, my dad slipped out of the picture entirely. That was a double dose of unexpected news, which meant I had to grow up fast. Mom had to apply for government assistance and go on welfare. It was *that* bad.

My new brother, William Dawson, was born on December 30, 1971. With Dad out of sight, I felt more like a father figure to William than an older brother, and I did what I could to help. Needing money more than ever, I got hired as a dishwasher working nights at the Forum Cafeteria in downtown Cleveland throughout the 11th and 12th grades.

One night after work, I narrowly avoided disaster. I was riding with some fellas in a stolen car littered with marijuana. The police pulled us over, and I pushed the weed between the seats while telling the cop that I didn't know the vehicle was stolen. Scared as you know what, I also told the officer the driver asked me if I needed a ride home, which is why I got in. Since it was a stolen car, I was taken to the police station, where I avoided trouble because I was able to hide the marijuana. Thankfully, I didn't have a record.

During my senior year at Shaw High School, I knew there was a chance I wouldn't graduate. My grades were just too bad, and my focus was even worse, so I had to take night classes and attend summer school. An example of how bad my academics had deteriorated was the fact I flunked the first semester of Black History. My teacher, Ms. Shahid, said to me, "Wayne, you should be ashamed of yourself." The following semester, I got an A, giving me a C in the class for the year. Looking back, this was the turning point of my life as a student, because it reminded me of the greatness within myself.

Still, I failed a couple of math classes, which required me to attend summer school, proving the strategy of doing just enough schoolwork to "get by" was a bad habit to develop. I don't advise anyone to follow that behavior because I was lucky to graduate in 1973—barely.

Once I was done with high school, I wasn't even considering college because I just wanted to work. The guys I hung out with during that time have now fallen off the map for the most part. Many of them are still getting high, and some are dead, so it wasn't only a bad path then, but it still is now.

Maybe I was spared because I didn't get into that life as deeply as they did, and I eventually got a job washing dishes at Lutheran Medical Center on West 25th Street.

But lo and behold, I was still corrupt in my mind, and I hooked up with the daughter of the biggest dope dealer on Cleveland's near westside. There was a housing project across from my job, and I soon faded over to the projects to hang out with that group. This behavior continued for about a year after I graduated.

During that entire time socializing, my friend Cortez was always in my ear saying things like, "Man, I don't know about you, but in ten years, I'm gonna be in the NBA, and you're gonna still be hangin' around with these guys doing the same thing they're doing now." But in the back of my mind, I always knew I wanted to do something with my life, no matter how off-track I was. I still knew what my mother had taught me, and I always believed in myself.

I hate to admit it, but once high school was over, I started selling drugs—nothing major, just marijuana. I would buy enough of it for me to smoke and sell the rest. One time, Mom found a half-pound of marijuana in my belongings, and she went off.

I think that's what broke me, and I stopped doing it. I'm not proud of that, but it's part of my existence and who I was back then. I praise God that I never went to jail for my juvenile behavior.

Looking back, my saving grace was deciding to go to college because I was tired of washing dishes at the hospital and didn't want to do that for the rest of my life. I wasn't sure what I could do, but I did like sports, so maybe I could be a sports reporter for a newspaper. My grades were so bad in high school that I had to take remedial math and English to get into Cuyahoga Community College.

## Takeaways from Chapter 2

### by Deante Young

Reading "Chapter 2: Reckless," I'm reminded of Ephesians 6:10-18 as I digest the trajectory of Wayne's life during the years 1967–1973.

That scripture talks about using the full armor of God to protect yourself against the devil's schemes. During his final year of middle school and throughout high school, Wayne was in the clutches of the enemy.

It surely didn't help that his family dynamic was fracturing day by day, helping to create a disconnect between young Wayne and his previously impenetrable dedication to academic supremacy.

But it was mostly the ill-advised choices that the newly adolescent Wayne made that undermined the esteemed values he'd been raised with as he decided to "hang out" with a rag-tag group of delinquents.

It must not be ignored that during those final years of the Civil Rights Movement, the country faced critical times, especially black folks in the inner cities.

As Dr. King's non-violent pleas for peace ended in his assassination and the Black Power movement grew in scope, Wayne found himself behaving recklessly and on a path of self-destruction.

But he also developed a positive self-image due in part to the achievements of notable black people. Both music and politics helped to fuel Wayne's pride in his race as he steadily grew into a young man.

I believe that he needed all the good, bad, and ugly of this period to grow into who he would eventually become. If we take the lessons from the experiences, the trials and tribulations are well worth it in the end.

# Chapter 3

# He Ordered My Steps

*We can make our plans.*
*But the Lord determines our steps.*
—Proverbs 16:9

It killed me to see Mom dealing with so much in the aftermath of Dad leaving. It's probably one of the reasons that I saw myself as a father figure to my brother William, yet I knew that I had to get on with my life. Dad and I kept in contact after he moved out, and he never had much advice to give. We always bonded over sports, but anything else was probably asking too much. It was such a relief to pass the twelfth grade thanks to summer school, and I was determined not to slack off on my studies ever again.

I believe that after the Lord saw this change in me and my renewed focus, He worked in His mysterious ways to help me get into college. We had fallen on hard times financially since Dad left, which is why we were on welfare and receiving food stamps. It was during this time Mom went back to school herself.

Because our household income was so low, I qualified for grants to pay for school.

Once I went further in my college career, I was approved for food stamps and textbook vouchers in later years at Kent State University. First, I attended Cuyahoga Community College (Tri-C), and God used the negativity of my father's departure to enable me to go to school almost debt free.

I will always believe that God was ordering my steps, and I didn't even know it at the time. When I look back on it, I know it had to be the hand of the Lord because it all just worked out.

Once I entered my freshman year at Tri-C in the fall of 1974, it was a whole different ball game, and my life completely changed. I focused on my goal to become a sportswriter because I liked sports and I had a gift for writing. Subsequently, I started writing for the college newspaper and eventually for the *Call and Post*, an African-American-themed newspaper based in Cleveland. I was finally starting to turn things around for myself and began acting and moving with a purpose.

I chose Tri-C partly because I didn't feel ready to go to a four-year school, especially after all the extra work I had to do just to graduate from high school. I also selected Tri-C's Metro campus because my friend Cortez, who had been a star basketball player at Shaw High School, was enrolled there. I became the sports reporter at Tri-C, allowing me to cover his exploits on the basketball court, which I loved doing.

My first year at Tri-C was my introduction to journalism, and I enjoyed it more each day. I networked with the athletes and coaches and used what I learned to craft sports stories beyond just basketball. I felt like a real-life reporter and publishing my articles in the school newspapers made it more of a reality for me. Finding and developing stories and the ins and outs of getting them published helped me understand the importance of preparation and being goal oriented.

I've said it many times, but it bears repeating; God will put people in your life to help you on your journey. Looking back, I can see how the great support and encouragement from my friend Cortez and my instructors at Tri-C were instrumental in molding me for future success.

It was incredible how much my life had changed by the start of 1975. I was fast approaching my 20th birthday and happier than ever. But more surprises were coming my way that would cause me to take all aspects of my life more seriously.

My girlfriend Sharon Holley, whom I met in 10th grade, was pregnant with our child. That breathtaking news was one of the main reasons that I turned my life around. The reality of having a daughter made me realize that it was time to stop playing.

Several of my old classmates and friends had babies or were pregnant at the time, so I knew that possibility existed for us. When Sharon told me the news, I was very happy she and I were going to be parents.

Tamara Cherise, our baby girl, was born on July 30, 1975, and shortly after that, my dad said to me, "I don't even know why you're going to school, you're a father now, and you need to get a job." For me, that went in one ear and out the other because I was not only proud to be a father, but I was determined to make it work.

Being a new dad was also one of the reasons why I got a job as a porter at the Eastern Star Home and worked there every summer and every school break during my college years.

It had been years since I was enthusiastic about school, but that's exactly what I was during my time at Tri-C. I was there for about a year and collected an impressive portfolio of my sports clips and writings that I knew would eventually add credibility to my skills. Cortez had received a full scholarship to Kent State University, and I decided to transfer there to expand my education and hopefully continue my quest to become a sportswriter.

I showed up at Kent during the fall quarter towards the end of '75 armed with my sports articles from Tri-C and the *Call and Post*. I headed to the school newspaper office and showed the folks there my portfolio. They basically said, "We have no room for you right now. Come back next year."

I must say, the Holy Spirit is powerful. I wasn't in touch with the Lord then, but He had His hand on my life, and I didn't know it because I was just doing me. But something told me to go over to the Music and Speech building. Mind you, I had never done any broadcasting in my life. I was a kid from the eastside of Cleveland and the king of Ebonics, but I walked over there, and they told me there was a slot for me and offered me the opportunity to do the sports report.

That's how my broadcasting career began. I started doing sports reporting on the campus radio station, became interested in TV, and the rest is history. I fell in love with broadcasting and returned to being an A student.

After being rejected by the school newspaper at Kent, something inside me said, "Try broadcasting." I don't know what it was, but it's probably because I just wanted to do journalism in any form, and broadcasting came to mind. When I was a kid, I would play imaginary games and mimic the roar of the crowds while doing the "play-by-play." That was the closest I had ever been to any sort of broadcasting.

In retrospect, I know it was the Lord guiding me through that without me knowing He was. I could've easily gone back to my dorm after being rejected by the school newspaper and sulked, lit a joint, and forgotten about it.

Even though I never envisioned a life in broadcasting, I was inspired by a few legends in the industry. The first broadcaster to inspire me was Bill Jacocks, a weekend anchor on Channel 5. I thought he was so cool. Another local broadcaster, Leon Bibb, inspired me, and on the national scene, a newsman by the name of Max Robinson.

Once I started the process of becoming a broadcaster at Kent, I began to focus on that. I would visualize myself working at a TV station because radio was no longer my goal once I got turned on to TV. I saw radio as a stepping stone to TV because when I was at Kent, I worked as a beat reporter at WKNT, a commercial radio station (it's called WNIR now). I covered the city council and did a public affairs show for Kent, Ravenna, Stow, and Akron.

I poured all of myself into broadcasting at Kent; I was the anchor and reporter along with being the news director. There were many days when I had to write the entire show because nobody else was around, and that really developed my writing skills. I was the news director and the anchor of TV2 for two years, and it prepared me well for a career in professional television.

I stayed at Kent for four years, and when I graduated in 1979, I was a realist. I sent my tapes to TV stations without getting any responses. I even did a couple of interviews, and folks were like, "Um yeah, ah…we'll get back with you."

## Takeaways from Chapter 3

### by Deante Young

If the collapse of Wayne's parents' marriage was the instigator of his descent into poor grades and worse behavior, then the hard-won lessons from those trying times were also responsible for the strength and resilience he carried during the early years of adulthood.

As I consumed the written recollections of Wayne Dawson's life during 1973-1979 in "Chapter 3: He Ordered My Steps," I was fascinated by how often Wayne handled adversity with poise and maturity.

Many people never get to meet their father for one reason or another, which can have a debilitating effect on a young child and adolescent.

Wayne not only knew his father, but also lived in the same household and saw his parents together for many years.

His father's gradual disappearance from the home might've dealt a bigger blow to young Wayne than if he'd never known his dad. That circumstance—the separation from his father and its effects on his mom— exacerbated Wayne's difficult transition from a teenager to an adult.

Making matters worse, Wayne's dad left soon after fathering a child with his mom. The searing pain that enveloped Annie Dawson's life at that time was bad enough, but Wayne suddenly found himself balancing a careless lifestyle with his so-called buddies and fighting to graduate high school—all while being a father figure to his baby brother.

To Wayne's credit, he recaptured his previous academic prowess while helping his mom through that very challenging time. And if the unexpected hardships that had already occurred weren't enough, Wayne then discovered that he would soon be a father to his own child!

Instead of reacting to that life-changing news with a negative outlook, he used it as another reason to acquire a greater level of focus to reshape his life.

I was also deeply inspired and awestruck at how fiercely dedicated he was to building his professional reputation in college to prepare for the career he was destined to have.

Finally, the biggest message any of us can take away from those critical years of Wayne's journey is that God will strategically place obstacles and the necessary people and circumstances in our lives to help us to fulfill our purpose.

Wayne has consistently expressed his unrelenting faith in our Heavenly Father because of the way that He ordered his steps to bring him where he needed to be.

I believe we can now truly understand why.

# Chapter 4

# To Whom Much is Given, Much is Required

*You cannot do a kindness too soon,*
*for you never know how soon it will be too late.*
—Ralph Waldo Emerson

At Kent State, the Lord put another important person in my path—April Sutton—a very aggressive lady and an obvious go-getter. She landed an interview with Virgil Dominic, a legend in the broadcasting business and the news director at WJKW-TV (now WJW) Channel 8 in Cleveland, Ohio.

"I have a friend at Kent State who is excellent! His name is Wayne Dawson," April said to Virgil.

Virgil's response: "Well, have him give me a call!"

I called Virgil, and he told me to bring him some of my work so he could check it out. I gave him my tape, he saw something in me and he put me in The Minority Training Program. Once again, God put April Sutton in my life at that time for that situation, and the rest is history. If she had not mentioned my name, I probably would never have ended up at Channel 8.

Pretty girls can open any door, and she was getting interviews all over the place, including Channel 8. Once she mentioned my name, we were both at that station. Virgil was in charge of hiring people for the news, and when I was hired in October 1979, it was near the end of Affirmative Action in the United States.

We had a union called AFTRA (American Federation of Television and Radio Artists), and the Minority Training Program was established to find more black broadcasters. I was lucky enough to get into that program, and it developed into a job. I started with Channel 8 at the end of '79, and initially, I was just observing how things were done.

The program kicked off at the beginning of 1980, and I went into the field with reporters three days a week. On the weekends, I would go out with the reporters and earn the chance to do news stories. Kent State prepared me very well for the journey that awaited me at *Newscenter 8* (the branding given to the newscasts) because I took on everything at Kent. I had to write all the stories, and we put on two newscasts per day, with me handling news director, producer, and anchor duties—a one-man band.

When I got to Channel 8, I was like, "Man, I can do this!" I had a positive attitude because I felt like I was in my element. My "official" start was in January 1980, and my first story was on the air about three weeks later. I would go out with a guy named Pete Carey, one of my mentors. I admired him because he was the first black news reporter in the city of Cleveland.

He was hired because of the Glenville riots, and the station needed a black presence to handle those stories. By that point, he had fallen out of favor with management and had to work weekends. So, he would take me out in the field with him, and he'd do his story, I'd do mine, and the station would put them on the air. Three weeks after graduating from Kent, there I was appearing on TV in Cleveland, the ninth-largest market in America at the time, and folks were like, "Whoa, how did that happen?"

Especially shocked at this very unlikely accomplishment were my old classmates at Kent. April Sutton and I were off and running in our new careers in television as the doors of opportunity swung open, and we took full advantage. I had done so much work at Kent that I was comfortable in front of the camera and knew how to write, so my mindset was "bring it on" because it all came naturally to me.

That happens when you prepare yourself for whatever you're attempting to do. I put everything into it and was focused on working hard, but I also visualized myself working at a TV station before it became a reality. I set goals for myself back then, and I still do. I put them on my mirror and recite them every morning, and amazingly, they eventually come true.

April was full of personality and wanted to be an entertainment reporter and interview celebrities. I just wanted to be the best reporter I could be, and we pursued our dreams relentlessly. She ended up going to Houston, Texas, before eventually carving out a hugely successful career in Hollywood that has lasted several decades, but her impact on my journey is everlasting.

One of the most important people I've ever met in my broadcasting career was Herb Thomas. I met him on my first or second day at the station, and fans of the Cleveland-based show *Big Chuck and Little John* know who he was. Herb portrayed the "Soul Man" character on that show, but he started working as the studio photographer at Channel 8 right out of high school. He produced a piece called *Meditations* that aired right before the TV signed off. For you youngsters out there, television didn't air content 24 hours a day back in the day, and Herb was the man that was partly responsible for signing us off with motivation and positivity.

Herb had an even greater significance in my life, and it started when I was training to be a reporter, and he was being trained to be a news photographer, a promotion from his job as a studio photographer. Think about that: we were often in the same car training for positions for which we would eventually win numerous awards.

Soon, Herb and I became known to some as the "dynamic duo." Anytime there was a story to be done in the inner city, we did it because we had the right contacts. We knew where the dope dealers, crackheads, and "strawberries" (prostitutes) were, and back in the day, we also knew where the "number runners" were. That insider information allowed us to dig up stories other people couldn't.

I worked with a lot of people, but Herb was my guy and the person I enjoyed collaborating with the most. Years later, we did a "public affairs" show called *Neighborhood* for Channel 8. We had no idea how blessed we were to be given 30 minutes per week to do whatever we wanted to do with that show. Herb and I, two black guys from Cleveland's inner city, had earned the trust required to be given freedom by the station to produce a show for the air without restrictions.

*Neighborhood* lasted about twelve years and won several Emmys, which was emblematic of our partnership and chemistry. Herb and I did so many stories together over many years—including the year that I was chosen to do a one-on-one interview with President George H.W. Bush.

Herb was such a wonderful photographer and friend. We worked together for 37 years before he retired. He passed away in 2021 and is now taking pictures as the chief photographer in Heaven.

Getting back to the start of my career, I kept climbing the mountain in Cleveland with *Newscenter 8* since being hired as a trainee in 1980-81. Then they hired me as a freelance reporter because there were no regular positions. In 1982, I was finally hired as a full-time reporter, and I've been there ever since.

Virgil Dominic was promoted to the general manager position, and Tony Ballew stepped in as my second news director. I was told that I spoke with a "black dialect," and the station sent me to a speech therapist at Case Western Reserve University. In my opinion, I *still* have a black dialect, but I guess back then, it was too black. Either way, the company paid for it, and I went through the training.

I'm not sure what I learned from it, or maybe I did learn something from it subconsciously, but whatever the case, they wanted me to sound more acceptable to middle America.

People often ask me how I dealt with fame in those early years, but the truth is simple: I never really thought about it because I was so focused on being the best I could be in my career. I never got caught up in adulation from the public. It's like, "Hey, you're on TV," but it just went in one ear and out the other because I know I could be here today and gone tomorrow. If you're off TV for a month, it's like, "Who cares?"

I always tried to be nice to people who recognized me and thanked them for watching *Newscenter 8* or Fox 8, but I never developed an ego, which helped me. I was always level-headed because I was just happy to be there and felt that it was a blessing.

When I started at *Newscenter 8*, I did not want to stay in Cleveland. My goal was to work in Washington D.C., but I didn't want to do "network" or anything like that. I just wanted to work there, so I went back and forth to D.C. during my first year at Channel 8, dropping off my tapes at different stations and staying with my relatives there.

I asked my family members questions about the area, and they told me about the cost of living, which made me feel like it was something to think about. But one thing led to another, and I kept getting promoted at Channel 8, so I got comfortable. One time I had the chance to go to Milwaukee, but I decided not to do it.

Considering my promotions at *Newscenter 8* and the cost of living in D.C. compared to Cleveland, I said, "I think I'm good just staying put." I also had my family and my daughter Tammy here in the city, so I made Cleveland my home and never thought about leaving after that.

The unique thing about my broadcasting career is that I have been at one station for 43 years: 40 years as an employee, one year as a trainee, and two years as a freelancer. 43 uninterrupted years on the air at one station must be some kind of record for a broadcaster in Cleveland. Others have been on the air longer than I, but they went back and forth between multiple stations. My 43 *consecutive* years at Channel 8 have been a blessing.

One reason the station was able to hire me full-time in 1982 was that a black reporter named Mattie Majors left. That opened a position for me and allowed Virgil to pay me the AFTRA minimum at the time. I worked Monday through Friday as a reporter doing all kinds of stories, and every so often, I was allowed to fill in an anchor position on weekends and holidays. But for the first ten years or so, I was just a reporter. In those early days at *Newscenter 8*, I had the good fortune of being around and learning from several broadcast journalists like Tim Taylor, Stan Childress, Bill McKay, Gary Stromberg, and Neil Zurcher.

I told veteran meteorologist Dick Goddard and anchorman Dave Buckel, "Man, I used to watch you guys growing up!" It's crazy to me when people see me now and say, "Man, I used to watch you on TV!" I was also a fan of Judd Hambrick, who was the primetime anchor around the time I showed up. I read about him and his brothers John and Mike while I was in college, and he was the consummate anchorman.

During this early point in my career, I was always trying to gain an edge any way that I could. In 1982, a man named Victor Hill recruited me to join Phi Beta Sigma, a historically black fraternity that was founded on the Howard University campus in 1914. Being a member of a fraternity is all about the contacts that you can make. I had studied the organization during my years at Kent State, but it was "grind time" for me while I was there so I didn't have much time to pledge or do anything besides my work.

I saw it as more of an association of men who encouraged one another if anyone was looking for a job referral and things like that. Once I joined,

I saw that its membership was made up of mostly professional men who did good in the community.

Even now, it's a group atmosphere, which is something I've never really gotten into, but the camaraderie among the Sigmas is outstanding.

Also early in my career, I began receiving invitations to speak at elementary schools all around Cleveland. I would always talk to the kids about "the ABCs of success" or being your "own best friend" or your "own worst enemy." Considering the position I was in at that time, my job was to inspire and motivate young people while letting them know that if I could do it, they could do it. My message to young people was to buckle down, focus, and set goals.

It's funny, but I run into young people today, grown men and women who say to me, "Man, you spoke at my fourth-grade class," and I say, "Really?" while looking up at them, and they're six foot two. It's a great feeling when someone comes up to me and says, "Man, I remember what you said when you spoke to me when I was in the fifth grade." Now they're grown with kids. It amazes me now to think about the many schools that I spoke at and even a few Boy Scout troops.

Speaking to students was my way of giving back in those days. I've always felt that to whom much is given, much is required or expected, so that's what I did.

I would only decline an invitation if I was out of town or had a scheduling conflict on that day. If they wanted me to come to speak, I'd find a way to make it, especially for young people.

Engaging with them was always satisfying for me, and I also felt very fortunate about my growing career. But in the news business, we often report stories so terrible that our human emotions come out, and it's difficult to be indifferent. On March 6, 1982, not long before I became a full-time reporter, a senseless tragedy hit the neighborhood where I spent my teenage years, East Cleveland.

On Ardenall Avenue, a man named Reginald Brooks killed his three sons as they slept and he then went into hiding. Several days later, he was caught by the police somewhere on the west coast, but the hard truth remained; this man shot his own kids in the head as they slept just to "get back" at his wife. What I soon discovered was that two of the sons were friends of my brother William.

I was at the station when the story was assigned to me. Keep in mind that this was my third year working at Channel 8, and the crime happened just two streets away from where I grew up. So, you can imagine how this situation played out in my mind. I covered the story, talked to the police, and talked to neighbors—but I couldn't bring myself to knock on that door to talk to the boys' mother.

For that reason, I chose to leave that out of my story.

When I got back to the station, I looked up at the televisions in the newsroom, and there she was on Channel 3. There she was on Channel 5, crying her eyes out, and I didn't have anything from her because I didn't knock on her door. That tragedy took place more than 40 years ago, and it still crosses my mind, but I know that I learned a lot from what I *didn't* do.

A more well-known Cleveland story is the 1984 rape and murder of 14-year-old Gloria Pointer. It was another senseless act of violence that I hated to see, especially as the father of a young daughter myself at the time. The Pointer murder is how I met a woman named Yvonne, Gloria's very strong and resilient mother.

In the decades since, Yvonne has become a dear friend. More importantly, she has kept her daughter's memory alive and has become an activist and advocate for violent crimes against children. Yvonne Pointer also opened a school in Africa in Gloria's name and has served countless children with her dedication to that very important cause.

Of course, not all the stories I've covered have been bad. Herb Thomas and I covered the first celebration of when Dr. Martin Luther King Jr.'s birthday became a national holiday. I've covered two Republican National Conventions. I also did a show called *Life's Work* for five years. I really enjoyed doing it because it focused on people and their passions.

It's not lost on me that my success in broadcast television is rare, especially for African-Americans. I've been asked if I ever experienced racism during my long career, and honestly, I've seen it, but I never internalized it. I never used racism as a crutch because I was too busy trying to be the best "me" I could be. I figured if I did that, somehow, the doors would open.

We can look at any situation and say that it should be better. But all in all, I think we've made great strides in TV in Cleveland. I've had two black female news directors who were both very good, so I really can't say much about discrimination. By the time I got into the business in 1980, things were looking up for people of color. There were black anchors on the evening news, and Channel 5 had a black general manager (he tried to recruit me to go there), although he's in Philadelphia now.

Some years later, another black woman was a general manager at Channel 19, and she also tried to get me to go there. So, I've seen blacks in decision-making positions, and partly because of that, I never felt discriminated against.

And we must remember that in the 80's, blacks were popping up on TV everywhere. In D.C., only brothers and sisters (black folks) were on the air, and it was the same in Detroit. Even here in Cleveland, I grew up watching Leon and Bill Jacocks, Kathy Adams and Mattie Majors.

Another one of my mentors was a reporter named Stan Childress, and I would watch him when I was a cub reporter. He broke it all down to me and said, "Wayne, there are only four elements in a news story: the soundbite, natural sound, the interview, and the voice track. It's how you manipulate those elements that make the story." He's no longer in the business, but I learned so much from him.

My personal life took an interesting turn in 1985. As my career as a reporter was flourishing, Sharon told me that she was pregnant again. It was happy news for me, and by that point, we had been living together for so long that we were, in a legal sense, common-law married.

We already had Tammy and knowing that I was going to be a new father again was a beautiful thing. Our second daughter, Crystal Monique, was born July 29, 1985, just one day before Tammy's tenth birthday. Ain't that crazy? It was the kind of good news I needed to balance out some of the nonsense that the world can throw at you.

Being a reporter for so many years was a great experience for me because I was able to get down in the weeds and encounter people from all walks of life on their best and worst days. But all the toiling and dedicating myself to becoming the best version of myself paid off when I became an anchor on weekend mornings in 1992 and worked briefly with a woman named Rebecca Shaw.

Soon after, I co-anchored with Robin Meade, who eventually went national with Headline News, and she's still there. We did weekend mornings together for about a year before I was promoted to weekend nights, and I did that for about six years.

People were happy about my promotion and felt as I did—that it was well deserved because I had paid my dues. During those early years anchoring, I worked with many talented individuals, and once I was switched to weekend nights, Kelly O'Donnell and I became a team. Like Robin

Meade, she later became a national journalist and a White House corre-spondent. She is currently a political reporter for NBC News.

When she left Channel 8, I worked with Laurie Jennings, and from there, my list of co-anchors continued to expand including Donna Davis and Kathy Kronenberger. Historically speaking, Donna Davis (who is now deceased) and I were Cleveland's first full time African-American anchor team.

Virgil had also made another great hire a couple years before that—a young woman from Alliance, Ohio named Stefani Schaefer, who we call "Sissy," and she also became one of my co-anchors on the weekend evening show.

Virgil always had an eye for talent and believed in giving inexperienced people a shot if he saw something in them; I was just one of the many people he hired. The list of individuals that Virgil Dominic has helped or discovered is long, from Kelly O'Donnell, Mike DiPasquale and Vince Cellini to Tana Carli and, of course, April Sutton. He just had a knack for recognizing talent.

When I began anchoring the weekday morning show with Stefani, our chemistry was obvious because we were like brother and sister. She event-ually went to work briefly with Bill Martin (though we teamed up for two more stints in later years), and I had a new co-anchor named Jackie Smith.

For the record, I wasn't the first black man to anchor the morning show. That distinction went to Rick Young, who started with Denise Dufala, Andre Bernier, and Dan Coughlin.

During that time, the station aired a program called *Interview* which I took part in, along with the public affairs show I mentioned before, *Neighborhood,* with Herb Thomas.

As my career reached new heights and my responsibilities increased, I never allowed any of it to spill over into my personal life. One of my gifts is the ability to compartmentalize, which helped me tremendously because if I was going through something at home or work, I could tune it out and focus on where I was at the moment.

The early 90s were an interesting time in my life. My daughter Tammy was transitioning into womanhood as her high school years ended. My daughter Crystal was still a kid, and both were the most important people in my life.

Still in my late 30s, I took full advantage of the blessings God placed in my life; a great career in television, my girls, and the freedom I enjoyed in living a bachelor's lifestyle part-time while still living with Sharon.

It might've been a blessed life, but the Lord was ready to open my eyes again.

## Takeaways from Chapter 4

### by Deante Young

As I studied the fascinating details of Wayne Dawson's transition from Kent State graduate to his virtually unprecedented rise to professional reporter, one key attribute of his stood out to me.

He had sown the seeds of greatness for years, and when the time was right, he reaped the fruits of his labor—selflessly and consistently. The appropriately titled fourth chapter, "To Whom Much is Given, Much is Required," opens with the burgeoning journalist on the precipice of success, and with the hand of God steering his journey, he was repeatedly rewarded for finally getting focused on improving his lot in life.

Wayne had stumbled to the finish line of his high school years with grades that impressed almost no one. But the five-year period between 1974 and

1979 produced a brand-new Dawson, uncompromising in his vision of fostering the career of his dreams and building a great life for his unexpected child.

Challenges and setbacks within his family and himself served as blessings in disguise because he had gotten his act together and *deserved* success. His mother received welfare, which enabled him to attend college for practically nothing.

The enormous responsibility of being a new father at 20 elevated his determination. The relentless polishing of his skills led to his being an undeniable talent, and it attracted the attention of a key decision maker named Virgil Dominic.

His giving heart enabled him to be rewarded time and time again with an increasingly higher income and privileged lifestyle. His charismatic personality never included ego or arrogance, earning him praise and respect for what he has represented.

For 43 years.

He always chose humanity over indifference when meeting people during their worst moments. As he traversed the complicated and rocky terrain of a broadcasting career and the celebrity that came with it, he remained a decent, down-to-earth human being.

While some co-anchors went on to more prominent positions in the U.S. media market, Wayne Dawson decided to stay put. He never sought out the bright lights or the admiration from the public. He just wanted to be the best that he could be, and *that* decision is why God continues to shower him with blessings.

Respect.

# Part II: An Unbroken Vessel?

By the time the new millennium arrived, Wayne Dawson had evolved to become a committed husband, a doting father and a studious practitioner of living his life through Christ.

For those reasons, I question whether Wayne could still be considered a "broken vessel," as he is known to call himself. This section of his wondrous journey delves deep into his most rewarding achievements as a man of faith. His 1997 marriage to LaVerne Reed was both surprising and predestined because of the transformative symmetry they shared as people who had "been through life."

That union helped to pave the way for Wayne's most profound challenge: answering God's call to become a man of the cloth. It was LaVerne's unwavering support and Wayne's willingness to ignore his fears and dedicate himself to the calling of a lifetime that made it become a reality.

This section also spotlights the philanthropic Annie L. Dawson Foundation, named to honor the great woman who birthed Wayne and his brother, Judge William, and it examines the incredible pride Mr. Dawson has in being a father of four children and grandfather of eight.

Let's dive in!

-D.Y.

# Chapter 5

# A Wife of Noble Character
# is Her Husband's Crown

*You are the finest, loveliest, tenderest,*
*and most beautiful person I have ever known*
*—and even that is an understatement.*
—F. Scott Fitzgerald

I had been living with Sharon since graduating from Kent State University in 1979, not just because she was the mother of my daughters Tammy and later, Crystal, but because we were in love. Sharon was very supportive in the early years of my television career. She and I were high school sweethearts, and we got engaged in the mid-1980s. I once heard that a lot of men, especially black men, don't get married because of a "fear of commitment," and ironically, we never tied the knot. However, we were together long enough to be considered "common-law married."

Looking back, I can see how different I was then, and it truly amazes me. I was wild with a "street mentality." I still wanted to run the streets but wanted a woman at home. As the old folks used to say, I wanted to "have my cake and eat it too!"

The spirit of the Lord was not in me because I had sold out to the world, and because of that, I never really settled down with Sharon. After many years together, she'd had enough and left me. I truly regret that our relationship fell apart and I take total responsibility for not being the best person I could be.

Throughout college and after I graduated and started working at Channel 8, Sharon was there for me as we navigated life together, me as an ambitious student and then a television reporter, and she as a postal worker. Despite all that, it didn't work out.

I am grateful to Sharon for handling that situation the way she did, and her level of understanding was exactly what I needed, but probably didn't deserve. I also thank God for His forgiveness, something else I didn't deserve.

During a brief period after my break-up with Sharon, I dated a young woman and fathered a child with her. My first and only son, Tyshin Dequan Dawson, was born on November 18, 1993, giving me three children at age 38. More on him later.

It's been said that God will turn a mess into a miracle, and that's exactly what He did in my life. Despite my unfaithfulness and checkered past, God gave me a second chance. Regardless of my imperfections and my weaknesses, God blessed me with another wonderful, God-fearing woman who became my wife.

God took the least likely in LaVerne and brought us together. Looking back, I can see God's hand guiding both me and LaVerne. Indeed, Proverbs 16:9 says, "*We can make our plans, but the Lord determines our steps.*" God directs and redirects our steps, and that's what He has done in my life, and I give Him all the glory. I truly believe God brought us together for His purpose, which was to become partners in the ministry.

Like myself, LaVerne has a story that is proof positive God can indeed use anyone for His glory. That's our story. We're now leading a church, and I could not have asked for a more willing and committed wife to be with me on this journey. It just goes to show you how God does what He does.

I also believe He connected us because we were available and had been through life by that time. As I said before, LaVerne has her own story, and I'm convinced God brought us together for a time such as this. It's all in His divine plan, and I understand that now, and whatever I went through before was preparing me for what I'm doing currently.

I'm humbled when I think about all that, and it sometimes brings a tear to my eye that God would use someone like me—a broken vessel—to represent Him. But once again, God uses the least among us so He can get the glory, and I'm the least among us because my life has not been pristine.

No one's life is flawless, and as my friend Deante Young talks about "the dirty truth" in his books, my life is full of *dirty-ness*. But God in His mercy dusted me off, and He's put me on the path to represent Him which is a blessing, and I can only thank Him for that.

LaVerne and I came from different worlds and met under the unlikeliest circumstances at a nightclub called, "The Reason Why." At the time, my thought process was, "This is just another lady I'll date, and have some fun." I quickly discovered something about her that kept me interested— she was an entrepreneur with her own beauty shop. That made me respect her because she wasn't just a girl out there kickin' it; she was a hard-working entrepreneur.

Somehow, after God brought us together, we grew together. Indeed, we could've walked away from each other many times, but that didn't happen. Now here we are, married for 25 years after dating for several years before that. I'm not dismissing Tammy and Crystal's mom because she is a wonderful woman and a great mother, and I loved her, but again, I was the one who ruined that relationship.

Have I been to jail? No. Was I a crackhead? No, but I was definitely on the other side of the tracks, and my life back then was morally corrupt. For God to use someone like me is proof that He can use anybody.

A key thing to remember is that I grew up when Blaxploitation movies were very popular. By the start of the 1970s, I was getting high and womanizing, and who did I look up to? Shaft, Dolemite, Superfly, and Iceberg Slim. Those guys were trendsetters and were glorified in the 'hood.

It was the thing to do, even though I didn't realize it was morally wrong. Films such as *The Mack* proved how jacked-up I was. I read *Pimp: The Story of My Life* about black pimps, which led to my desert experience. Being inundated with all those images in books, movies, and the pimp "heroes" in my community helped create a negative period in my life.

That "pimp mentality" permeated a lot of guys, making us want more than one girlfriend. It's not that those guys wanted the girls to sell their bodies, but the perception was, "If you're really *all that,* you've got to have more than one girlfriend." Mind you, those individuals became the parents of the next generation, which explains something I heard about our generation being the one that "dropped the ball." We were just past the Civil Rights Movement and we dropped the ball.

I'm glad the Lord allowed me to develop my spirituality because I now understand that, "We reap what we sow."

LaVerne Reed and I met in 1987, had breakups over the years, and I even dated other women. I didn't realize then that I was in a divine relationship with her. Something kept us together because God knew what He had planned for us.

By 1995, LaVerne and I were dating again, and little did I know that the next two years were about to prove to me just how much I needed her. My father and I had a lukewarm relationship until I got older. Once I was advancing in my career at Channel 8, we became a lot closer, even though he was mostly distant as I grew up.

Despite that, I always appreciated that he modeled the importance of hard work—both he and my mother were hard workers. Once I was grown, he was very proud of me and as I mentioned earlier, we kept in touch after he walked out on us many years before.

Dad had many jobs, most of them driving trucks and buses, and he eventually retired from the RTA. His final job was as an usher in the bleachers at the newly built Jacobs Field in downtown Cleveland. This was when the Cleveland Indians featured Albert Belle, Manny Ramirez, Kenny Lofton, Sandy Alomar Jr. and others, and because he was a big sports fan, it was Dad's favorite job.

Suddenly, he suffered a stroke and drove himself to the hospital. He lost the use of the left side of his body and when I visited him in the hospital, he was sitting on the side of his bed and apparently had another stroke. I remember asking, "Dad, what's up?" I didn't understand why he wasn't responding.

Soon after that, on October 16, 1995, I was in Washington D.C. with Herb Thomas covering the Million Man March and I received word that my dad did in fact have a second stroke. When he was released from the hospital, Mom brought him home and took care of him.

Almost 25 years after he walked away from us, when Mom was pregnant with my brother William, she brought Dad home and took care of him. That's wild. After a few months, we had to put him in a nursing home because it became too much for my mom to care for Dad at that point.

LaVerne was a huge support during all this, and it proved that God wanted her in my life for reasons we didn't fully understand at the time.

My eyes were really opened to that reality when my mom became very sick in 1996, and LaVerne became my rock. We had been dating seriously for a while, but once again, I was a bit hesitant about getting married. That's how a lot of young men are; they'll date someone although they're unsure they want to settle down and give up the single life. That's probably what was going on with me.

Mom had been sick for a long time, and nobody knew it because she suffered silently and never complained. It got so bad that she had to go to the hospital, where she learned she had diverticulitis, which is not a deadly disease—it's just a perforated intestine. However, she had let it go for so long that the poison infiltrated her internal organs.

After her first surgery, she was up walking and talking.

She had a second surgery the following week, and it seemed like she was "gone" because she never spoke again. Mom had surgery four consecutive weeks before she died on August 7, 1996, just five days before her 66th birthday, and it broke my heart. I thought about how we talked after her first surgery and then never communicated again because she was always out of it.

LaVerne visited my mother often at that time. She washed her hair and helped in any way she could even though Mom wasn't close to her. As far as my mom was concerned, LaVerne was just another woman I was dating.

To her credit, LaVerne stepped up and helped my mother and was there when I couldn't be. She is a nurturer, which was a big deal for me. My mother didn't know how serious my relationship with LaVerne was because she had seen me date other women, especially Sharon. Indeed, my mother's attitude about the women I dated was that if I *liked* them, she *loved* them.

When my mom passed, I felt a huge sense of loneliness. My daughter Tammy was older and moving on with her life, Crystal was too young to grasp what was happening, and Dad was in a nursing home. I think the Holy Spirit just buckled down and said, "It's time," and that led to LaVerne and I getting married a year after Mom left us.

I cut off all the other relationships I was involved in and have been loyal and monogamous ever since. We didn't have a big wedding; we were married by a pastor we knew on Friday evening, August 29, 1997, and left the next day for our honeymoon in Cancun.

I was 42 when LaVerne and I got married, and I admit that I feared commitment, but sometimes you just have to go for it, and that's exactly what I did. The first year of our marriage was rocky, and according to LaVerne, she was ready to leave a couple of times, but she hung in there. We started going to church, which became a big part of our lives and really helped our marriage.

The biggest contributor to the "rockiness" of the relationship during the first year was falling back on our old habits from when we were single. Once Sharon left me, I basically did what I wanted to do–until I married LaVerne.

Tragedy hit again on December 4, 1997, when Dad had another stroke at the nursing home and passed away at the hospital. LaVerne was there to comfort me yet again, just three months after we got married. Praise God for her because I needed her presence during times like that.

I didn't think our first year as a married couple was that bad, but LaVerne felt differently. I don't recall much turmoil, but I also have a way of suppressing things. LaVerne remembers everything, so I rely on her memory of that first year.

Maybe that's a defense mechanism for me. I don't concentrate on negative stuff; I let it go. I remember one time she said, "I was ready to leave, but Aunt Martha talked me off the cliff," I was like, "Really?" Praise the Lord for allowing us to correct course and getting us in church together, which stabilized our relationship.

During those early years of our marriage, we didn't think we could have any kids together. Of course, I had three kids before we got married, but LaVerne didn't have any, and once she hit her 40th birthday in 2001, it seemed even less likely to happen. God blessed us just a year later on January 24th, 2002, when Danielle, our first child together, was born after a rough pregnancy for LaVerne. I viewed this miracle as more than just a blessing; it also solidified our marriage and gave my wife a sense of worth and purpose.

The birth of this child, and in later years, LaVerne's willingness to be my partner in the ministry, strengthened us as a couple. When I talked to her about how the Lord had called me into the ministry and the step I was about to take, she told me that she was "all in," which was very encouraging.

That's all I needed to hear.

## Takeaways from Chapter 5

### by Deante Young

One thing I found quite striking in Chapter 5, "A Wife of Noble Character is Her Husband's Crown," is Wayne Dawson's high level of transparency. His brutal honesty, combined with an uncommon sense of self-awareness, is one of the key elements of his stunning transformation from "Casanova" to a monogamous man of God.

But much credit must be given to LaVerne, a woman he met at a nightclub during a season of his life when such an encounter would lead nowhere worthwhile. I believe that God organized that meeting between two souls who were predestined to fulfill a specific mission: to improve each other's lives and, eventually, serve His will as partners.

Unbeknownst to Wayne, he had been infected with the mental virus known as "toxic masculinity" as a young man, and LaVerne was the antidote for such behavior. No, their initial meet-up at "The Reason Why" nightclub didn't instantly lead to a fairytale courtship. But LaVerne's entrepreneurial ambitions at the time impressed Wayne enough to recognize that she was not some "around the way" girl.

He kept in touch with her because his instincts told him to. Years later, during the worst period of his life, Mr. Dawson witnessed the true essence of LaVerne. Now his girlfriend, she comforted both him and his beloved mother during her final days with an empathetic and heartwarming touch. The emotional weight of those dark days for Wayne led him to a new chapter in his personal growth, and he finally understood *the reason why* he kept in touch with LaVerne for years.

Soon after, he did what many of his closest friends believed impossible; he gave LaVerne his last name and tossed his old womanizing habits in the trash. He was open to allowing a woman to make him a better man, and that was made possible by Wayne first being self-aware enough to know that he didn't need a woman. He needed the *right* woman, and that's exactly who graced his life and became his crown.

# Chapter 6

# I Can Do All Things
# Through Christ Who Strengthens Me

*Man says... Show me and I'll trust you.*
*God says...Trust me and I'll show you.*
—Psalm 126:6

Even before I was married, I was asked to speak at various Men's Day events at churches around the city, and I did that a lot. Then something occurred to me: since I was already speaking at those church events, I probably should learn something about the Bible. For many years, I believed that God had a calling on my life because Stephen Rowan's father, the great Albert T. Rowan, kept pulling me into that world. He even appointed me a member of the trustee board at Bethany Baptist Church.

I started going to a seminary because Pastor A.T. Rowan opened the door to make me want to study and take classes. I received numerous invitations to speak at churches because that's what happens when you're on television. Some guys do it, and some don't. I spoke to many groups at that time as my way of giving back, something I learned from Eleanor Hayes, one of my former co-workers at Channel 8.

Following Eleanor's example, I learned to stay visible in the community to truly maximize my impact on people. Seeing how that was her key to success, it became my thought process.

She was always speaking at various schools or to groups, and because of that, the station respected her. I admired that a lot, so I made a point to be out there doing things in the community.

I had been taking seminary classes, and a lot of pastors would say, "Come on, I'll license you." Eventually, I spoke with a good friend of mine named Dr. John Walker Jr., whom I met here in Cleveland, but was now living in Jacksonville, Florida. He was a pastor and a good friend of Stephen Rowan's, who has been the senior pastor at Bethany Baptist Church since 1999.

"Look, man, you need to go back to Bethany and talk to Rowan," John said.

Of course, I knew Steve as a kid and looked up to him just as I looked up to his dad A.T. Rowan. John insisted that Steve was the person whose guidance I needed to be under. I soon had lunch with Steve and told him that I believed I had a call on my life. At that point, Steve took me under his wing, and from there, the process was slow. Steve is not a guy that does anything quickly. He really takes his time with stuff.

After a few years, he licensed me, and then on September 14, 2014, he ordained me at Bethany. I never said, "Hey Steve, when are you going to ordain me?" Many folks did that, but I just played it cool, and one day, he told me he felt I was ready to be ordained. Our relationship has always been based on friendship, and because of that, I viewed the times when we would visit the sick, do funerals and ministry work as hanging out. I was his associate and was there to support him.

I didn't realize God was also training me through him. The relationship grew and Steve's relationship with the late Reverend Dr. Jeremiah Pryce, who founded Grace Tabernacle Baptist Church in 1987, was the reason I was hired at Grace. No question, Steve's been very influential in my life when it comes to ministry work, and even now, he is a trusted confidant.

Before I got into the ministry, some of my best friends were pastors. I'm good friends with Bishop Joey Johnson, who heads the House of the Lord church, and I took my first seminary classes with him. He's been a good friend, good role model, great preacher, and man of God.

Pastor Kevin James is also a good friend and a wonderful example of what a true man of God is—not arrogant or self-serving. He's in the ministry for the gospel, not to glorify himself or to gain recognition, he just wants to do the right thing. These individuals have laid the foundation for me and what I want to be as a man of God.

Then there's John Walker Jr., the man I mentioned earlier whom I met when he lived in Cleveland while pastoring at Lane Metropolitan C.M.E church.

A lot of preachers are celebrity pastors, and I've always believed being that type takes some of the shine away from Jesus. He's the one that should get the shine, we're just his workers and His voice is "crying in the wilderness." This is just my philosophy, but I believe pastors need to take a back seat when it comes to their ministry, and Christ should be first and foremost. I'm not there to outshine Him or share "equal billing." He's the one that did all the work on the cross, and I'm just the messenger.

That's the way Pastor Rowan, Pastor Walker, Bishop Joey, and Pastor Kevin are, and that's why they have influenced me greatly. I also love the way Pastor R.A. Vernon has built his church, and he is good at preaching and teaching the gospel.

I think about what John the Baptist said: "I have to decrease so Christ can increase," and that's what I'm all about. The Bible talks about itching ears, which is to preach what people want to hear. People are not interested in hearing the true word, they're interested in hearing, "God's got a blessing for you" and "this is the year of jubilee."

I believe Dr. Martin Luther King Jr. was a man of God. I think he was anointed and was a modern-day apostle. I believe he came here to save black people, minorities and poor people, and when his job was over, God took him home. If you recall the night before he was killed, Dr. King said, "I've been to the mountaintop." That was prophetic, and it was what Moses said when he went to Mount Nebo.

Moses said, "I've been to the mountaintop," and God said, "I'll let you *see* the Promised Land, but you'll never get there." That was because of a sin he had committed, and that's the same thing that happened to King. He said, "I may not get there with you, but we as a people will get to the Promised Land." Then he was killed the next night.

Before I came back to Bethany Baptist Church after many years away, I was all over the place. I was studying Unity, which is something like a Christian Science philosophy, and then my wife told me about the House of the Lord in Akron, and I started going there. I was really tied in at the House of the Lord, and I was always there without ever officially joining the church.

That's where Bishop Joey Johnson spoke life into me. After that, I occasionally attended New Community Church before coming back to Bethany. It was familiar territory, of course, because I went there as a child. As I mentioned earlier, my grandfather was a deacon there, and we walked to church since it was just three blocks from our home on Drexel Avenue.

I was baptized as a child at Bethany by that young charismatic pastor I viewed as a role model, the Reverend Dr. Albert T. Rowan. In every way, Bethany will always be my home church. I attended the Trinity College of the Bible and Theological Seminary through distance learning, and I'm about to receive my Master's Degree in Biblical Studies. It was Albert T. Rowan that told me that I needed to take those courses and directed me to Trinity. Both he and his son Steve attended that seminary.

When I was ready to take the next step toward becoming a pastor, I received more advice than I could've ever imagined. But it was a blessing to receive it from people who were already doing what I was about to do. I knew for certain that the role of pastor would require a lot of energy and emotional resilience, and I felt ready to take on the challenge.

Because of Pastor Steve's friendship with Pastor Pryce, I was approached by Steve on Pryce's behalf once he took ill in 2016. He asked Rowan to ask me to consider stepping in at Grace as he worked to recover from his illness. Unfortunately, Pastor Pryce died in January 2017, which devastated longtime members of his church.

I officially became the interim pastor in July 2017, and about a year later, I was ordained as the new pastor of Grace Tabernacle Baptist Church. Through the grace of God, I've never felt overwhelmed in my position as pastor, and I think Grace is the perfect church for me.

In my opinion, the church runs itself, and I only provide a little direction here and there along with casting a vision. It's a great church, and Pastor Pryce laid a wonderful foundation that allowed me to move right in.

For the first year, there was a lot of infighting going on between different factions and hurt feelings because Dr. Pryce had been battling cancer for two years and he was often out of the pulpit.

When a pastor is not present in their church due to sickness or something else, the church sometimes goes in different directions, and that is what was happening at Grace.

Suddenly, Pastor Pryce was fighting his cancer, and the church became secondary. Many things were going on when I started at Grace as the interim pastor, and to God be the glory it worked out. I came in preaching love and unity and thankfully, my divinely-inspired messages began to take hold.

When it comes to pastoring, I'm totally dependent on the Lord because of my inadequacies. I've learned to depend on the Lord and to listen to His still, small, voice, which is His Holy Spirit. Indeed, I'm living my favorite scripture Philippians 4:13, "I can do all things through Christ who strengthens me."

Once again, I know my steps were ordered at Grace because I had no previous desire to be a pastor, but the doors just opened. I never feel stressed because I'm doing whatever God leads me to do, and that's what I try to do. I keep my feelings and agenda out of it, and I just try to follow whatever the spirit leads me to do. That's been my policy because I'm just the vehicle.

I'm God's hands, feet, and heart here on Earth, and if it were left up to me, I wouldn't know what I was doing because I was never prepared for this. Steve Rowan's dad was a pastor, so he knew what he was getting into. Dr. Vernon always wanted to be a pastor, so he knew what he was getting into. Many other men know pastoring because it's always been what they have done, but all I was trained to be is a journalist.

I came into this kind of blind because I didn't really know what I was getting into, and that was probably a good thing because if I had known, I probably would've said, "I'm good." Like I always say, it's not my church, it's God's church, and I'm just a vessel to help the people, love them, and lead them in the right direction.

In this position, I must meet people where they are and try to get the best out of them while doing it in a loving way. To me, it's been fun, and God bless LaVerne because she's been right there with me offering support, and I appreciate that. I make it a point to tell her that the Lord brought us together for a time such as this; that's probably why we hung in there through everything.

The fact that God brought us out of our checkered backgrounds for a time such as this, shows that He can use anyone, and it doesn't matter who you've been or what you've done. He can use anyone if you're willing to be used and our lives are a prime example. People look at LaVerne and can't believe that she's a First Lady, and they look at me and can't believe that I'm a pastor.

Once again, during my initial year at Grace as the official pastor, the first challenge was in bringing the people together because there was an emotional split. The death of their founding pastor left a very serious void, not only in leadership, but also in the infighting that I mentioned earlier. I was faced with having to bring the divided church together, and most of my sermons were about love and forgiveness.

Not only was it the first challenge, but it was a big challenge, and praise be to God we were able to get through that. Nothing is perfect, especially church because it's a reflection of the world, and we still have issues, but they're not as bad as they were. My strategy now is to navigate the personalities so we can move the church forward, and we've been blessed to do some wonderful things.

I can't take any credit for the food bank, the youth wing that's been totally redone, the media ministry, or the community outreach. It's a good church that provides blankets and hot meals during winter, but the people make it happen. All I do is say, "Hey, let's do this," and others jump on board and follow my vision, which is a beautiful thing.

At this point, it's all about giving back; that's why I don't mind helping the church financially wherever I can. God has blessed me with a wonderful career, a good wife, and a good family, so my purpose at Grace is to serve the Lord and His people for as long as He wants me to do that, which is the only reason I'm here.

I'm all about the spirit of giving at this point, and that's one of the reasons I can't say enough about the Annie L. Dawson Foundation that my brother William and I founded in 2007. We've always taken so much joy in giving back to the community, and I'm proud to be a part of it and the things we've done as a small foundation.

Establishing it was William's idea, and God bless my brother because he's always the initiator of great ideas. When he mentioned it to me, I was like, "Man, that's a great idea; let's roll." Of course, the fact that I'm in the media helped, but it was his idea, and we jumped on it. We named it after our mother because it was meant to pay tribute to her and the values she stood for; she was the neighborhood mother and would always tell people, "You can do it."

She put education first and told William and I that where she didn't succeed, we *would* succeed. She initially planted the seeds of greatness in me and inspired the positive affirmations that I recite every day. She had expectations for both him and I, and as long as she had control over us, she didn't accept anything less than our best.

We don't get big money from other major foundations, we only get donations here and there from people who like us. We've been able to do wonderful things with the scholarships and provide coats, shoes, hats, and gloves for the wintertime for kids. We also host the "Cycle Breakers" conference. Each year, William organizes it, and we speak life into high school kids and encourage them to believe they can do anything.

I'm proud of how the family has united to support and keep the foundation going. The Wayne Dawson Celebrity Bowl-A-Thon charity event that we used to host was a great endeavor. COVID shut us down for a couple of years, but we look forward to hosting it again because it is an excellent way to give back.

I just want to be a blessing to people because I have been blessed. Am I a highly paid, nationally known network anchor? No. But God has blessed me in Cleveland. He's allowed me to blossom here at home with my family in the place I grew up and to give back to a city that has given so much to me. Unlike other folks, I never left Northeast Ohio. I am truly one of "Cleveland's Own."

Even my college days were spent at nearby Kent, so I was still here in Northeast Ohio during those years. I'm a part of the fabric of the city, and I'm proud of that. There's nobody else in the history of this town that can say that—except maybe Dick Goddard.

I was born here, raised here, and never left here, and that's my story.

## Takeaways from Chapter 6

### by Deante Young

Most of us have the bad habit of finding problems in every opportunity, but Wayne Dawson is a man that finds opportunities in every problem. As I read Chapter 6, "I Can Do All Things Through Christ Who Strengthens Me," I was happy to learn that a sad occurrence became fuel for Wayne's personal development.

The unfortunate passing of the Reverend Dr. Jeremiah Pryce opened the door for Wayne to graduate from interim to full-time pastor at Grace Tabernacle. By that point, he had become fully entrenched in the idea that God had been leading him to that vocation for many years, and he initially served as a guiding light for a devastated church in transition. He met the challenge head-on despite having a full schedule with his broadcasting career and other community-based obligations.

Wayne has repeatedly referred to himself as a "broken vessel" who lived a life of sin for a long time. That fact alone makes his metamorphosis far more inspiring, especially because he practices what he preaches. Leading a church is not for the faint of heart, but it's a worthy undertaking when one's intentions are pure, which Wayne's certainly are.

That same spirit of giving also propelled him to join forces with his brother William to launch the Dawson Foundation in honor of their mother. Her values and sensibilities are the very fabric on which their foundation is built, and it further cements Wayne's legacy as that of a transformative figure.

It may go unnoticed, but Wayne always makes it a point to credit the willingness of his wife to join him on this spiritual journey as being the key to it working so well. LaVerne is an essential force of nature as First Lady of Grace Tabernacle. Without her and Wayne's partnership flourishing, many of us would miss out on an unlimited number of blessings.

# Chapter 7

# Children are a Heritage from the Lord

*The child is the beauty of God present in the world,*
*that greatest gift to a family.*
—Mother Teresa

Sometimes I think about the meaning of Psalm 127:3 and how it applies to my journey. The scripture reads, in part: "*Children are a heritage from the Lord, offspring a reward from Him.*" Indeed, nothing in this life matters more to me than my children and, by extension, their children. They're the center of my world, and even now, I'm putty in the hands of my daughters. I've always wanted to be there for them and let them know that no matter what happens in life or with their significant others, I will always be there. I'm a consistent presence, and they know that.

I was blessed with three beautiful daughters, Tamara Cherise (Tammy), born during my college years on July 30, 1975; Crystal Monique born just as my broadcasting career was taking off on July 29, 1985; and my baby girl, Danielle, born January 24, 2002. My ex-girlfriend Sharon is the mother of Tammy and Chris, and my lovely wife LaVerne is Danielle's mom.

No matter what they go through, and my two oldest daughters have gone through rough relationships and divorces, I've been there for them. Since all three of them were very young, I've told them that they will always have a man in their life who will look after them and take care of them.

My approach is the same way with Danielle. I don't know where I got that from, but it's just a fatherly love, and it's innate to be that kind of father and just be "Daddy." A father is the daughter's first male love, and it's important that men understand that.

Yes, she's going to love other men, but you, as the father, are the first, and that's a big responsibility. I've always wanted to model myself as a man they could be proud of and provide an example of the kind of man they should marry. I was a little hard on my daughters and had "discipline moments" when they probably didn't like me too much. No matter how much I kicked it with women in my younger years, my daughters were always number one for me.

During my single days, Tammy came to live with me, and she stayed there until I married LaVerne. With both of us grown, we occasionally went out to a few nightclubs and had a good time. I know she saw a new dimension of me during those moments, which happened at the very end of my single life.

As I mentioned in Chapter 5, I also have a son named Tyshin Dequan Dawson. He was conceived during a time when I wasn't with Sharon or LaVerne, and I was just kickin' it. I dated his mom Mctrena, and even now, he looks just like me. I'm very proud of the man Tyshin has become, and he also works in television as a producer in Birmingham, Alabama.

Sometimes I feel it's necessary to let folks know that I played an integral part in his life growing up, and LaVerne and my daughters have always loved him. He's a nice young man and doesn't have kids. When Tyshin visited Ohio during his college years, I occasionally brought him to the station, which I think helped to influence his career moves because all he knew as a kid was that I was on TV.

When he went to college, he majored in broadcast journalism. During the summers, I brought him back to Ohio and allowed him to shadow me at work so he could get a feel for the business. My limited influence over his life was powerful, and until he and his mom moved to Alabama during his 10th grade year, Tyshin had been a huge part of my life.

I hated missing his last three years of high school, but I continued to support him financially because I wanted him to have the best possible opportunities in life.

As much as I love my four children, I love my eight grandchildren just the same, and there's nothing I won't do for them. They range in age from toddler to adulthood, and I praise God for all of them. I'm the "come to me and ask me for anything, and you'll probably get it" guy.

I remember my mom used to always come over on Christmas Day. It was her favorite holiday and one of the highlights of my life with Sharon was on Christmas mornings when Mom would bring over a bunch of toys for Tammy and Crystal.

She arrived while they were still asleep because she wanted to be there when they awoke. As William and I were growing up, she always made sure our Christmas was great. Even though there were times we didn't have much, there was nothing I asked for that I didn't get for Christmas.

I believed that played a part in me doing the same thing for my kids and grandkids, and of course, she treated my kids like she treated me and William at Christmas.

My kids and grandkids are blessed because my mother's love for Christmas has rubbed off on me!

## Takeaways from Chapter 7

### by Deante Young

Wayne Dawson spent the better part of a quarter century skirt chasing and living a secular life with a seemingly endless assortment of women at his beck and call. But his marriage to LaVerne Reed in 1997 wasn't the only thing that was more important than a playboy lifestyle.

His children were his top priority 100% of the time, but he was understandably stricter with his girls.

As I read the touching words from Wayne in Chapter 7, "Children Are a Heritage from the Lord," I felt a profound sense of admiration for how he prioritized the young women that he helped to conceive, as well as his only son.

Considering the demands of his college years, during which time he was a hyper-focused student determined to succeed in the television business, he miraculously kept his toddler daughter Tammy as his single biggest concern.

That mindset continued as Wayne stepped into the pro ranks of broadcasting in late 1979 and kept on with the birth of his daughter Crystal just months after his 30th birthday. Nearly seventeen years later, after Mr. Dawson had long since ascended to legendary status in Northeast Ohio, his third daughter, Danielle, came into the world. In between the births of his second and third daughters was the birth of his son Tyshin in 1993.

The mentorship that Wayne provided his son as he gave him hands-on experience in broadcast journalism was enviable and heartwarming. It must also be acknowledged that Wayne Dawson lived outside the stereotypes and popular perception that black fathers are deadbeat dads.

He has always been a consistent presence in the lives of his children and is still happy to be there for them all. As he put it, he is "putty" in the hands of his daughters. I was also smitten with Dawson's unconditional love for his grandchildren and his willingness and eagerness to do anything for them.

Lastly, despite Wayne's treasure trove of accomplishments and the historic nature of his career, his crowning achievements will forever be the relationship he has always had with his children and grandchildren. The pride that he has held as a parent for nearly a half-century is both noble and inspiring.

Many of us wish we had a father like him.

# Chapter 8

# In the Middle of History

*Remember, no human condition is ever permanent.*
*Then you will not be overjoyed in good fortune,*
*nor too sorrowful in misfortune.*
—Socrates

During my four decades as a reporter and anchor, people have asked me numerous times about controversial moments on the air and history-making news stories. Here are my recollections of some of the most notable moments of my career in front of the camera.

## The 9/11 Terrorist Attacks (September 11, 2001)

Stefani Schaefer and I were on the air doing a regular show; then suddenly, we went "live" to New York because a plane had slammed into the World Trade Center. My first thought process is that it's an accident; somebody was flying too low, lost control, and the pilot went into distress and flew into the World Trade Center.

So, we immediately "took network" (Fox and CNN) and monitored the situation from the anchor desk. Then, we switched from the national networks for local reaction, which is when the second plane hit. At that point, we knew we were under attack, and Stefani and I were on the air at that time, trying to monitor what was happening while talking people through it as much as we could.

We kept going back and forth between New York and Cleveland. Soon, we learned that the Pentagon had been attacked and another plane went down in Shanksville, Pennsylvania.

We were thinking, "Oh my God. We're under attack," while trying to stay calm and be a voice of reason. I remember going home that day from the station fearful about what was happening like everyone else.

We didn't know what was going on.

I left the station and went to a Christian bookstore to get something uplifting to read.

In the days that followed, it had become an ongoing news story, but what stands out to me is the number of people who went to church during the weeks following the attacks. People were really coming to Christ because they just didn't know what to expect next.

America had been attacked, so a sense of fear remained.

## The "Skin Flute" Fiasco (June 17, 2007)

During the morning show with my co-anchor Tracy McCool, we were previewing a segment about a contest for air guitarists just as we cut to Fox 8's feature reporter Kenny Crumpton, who was on location doing his thing. Tracy said something about Kenny having the skill to play the air guitar, and off the cuff, I said that I had seen him play the skin flute.

I knew it was kind of off-color, but I didn't know *how* off-color it was.

Hand to God, I didn't know what a skin flute was. I had heard the term before, but I didn't know what it was. Folks started coming up to me asking, "Do you know what a skin flute is?" I replied that I didn't know what it meant. I later found out that it's a very popular term in Caucasian culture. A few blacks knew what it meant, but most had no idea.

I went on a scheduled vacation for a week right after the incident, and people thought I had been suspended by the station.

I'll never live that moment down.

## Barack Obama is Elected President of the United States (November 4, 2008)

This was the proudest day of my career. To hear Barack Obama had won that night, then go into the station the next morning and broadcast that "We have a black president!" I never thought it would happen.

When I came in at 4 AM the next morning, the smile on my face was incredible. Then, I was given the opportunity to cover his first inauguration on January 20, 2009, in Washington D.C.

That was a great moment for me because I was in D.C. among all the other reporters covering the inauguration of Barack Obama. I covered a couple of the presidential balls the night of the inauguration and handled the Ohio delegation. When he and the newly minted First Lady Michelle showed up, it was just a beautiful thing, and I was there to cover it.

I did live shots throughout the day and covered the event at night, and it instantly became one of the highlights of my career. Being in the midst of that history-making event as it happened, I was like, "Wow! We finally made it." That was the proudest I had ever been to be an American.

## The Rescue of Amanda Berry, Gina DeJesus, and Michelle Knight (May 6, 2013)

This was an unbelievable story! I wasn't on the air when it happened, but I came in the next day and did the story. My first reaction to the news that they had been found was, "God is good." After being missing for 10 years, most of us thought those girls were dead.

I wasn't on that story when they were found, but I wished I was. As a former reporter, when you hear stories like that, you want to leave the anchor desk and be a reporter again.

That's when you go right to the scene, in the midst of it all and interview people. It was incredible, and God bless them. I have so much respect for Amanda Berry for how she's pulled her life together after that, and I am proud to say she is a colleague.

It was crazy to learn that Ariel Castro, the guy who held those girls captive for over a decade, performed on Fox 8 with his band right around the time he kidnapped Amanda.

Who knew?

## The Human Experience

Life is crazy. Between the ministry and TV, I've seen it all. Life can be a mess, and people can be a mess, but it is what it is. I've seen parts of life that no one ever sees, and, in the ministry, I see various parts of people. I grieve with people, I'm happy with people, I marry them and bury them, so I've experienced the full gamut of the human experience.

Being in this life is like being in the muck with folks in the ministry and on TV. I take it personally when I see people going through the worst moments of their lives. When I'm talking with individuals dealing with tragedy, I try to be very sensitive in how I approach and deal with them, and God has always been with me.

Some reporters are not sensitive, and to them, it's just a story. For me, it's people dealing with real life.

## Kristi Capel Makes a Mistake (February 23, 2015)

What she said on the air didn't hit me until it was over. It happened so fast. I thought I heard it, but I wasn't sure. No one would say anything like that on the air if they knew what it meant. By that point, I knew Kristi's heart. Although she and I didn't pray together on the set, she and her family were there when I was ordained at Bethany Baptist Church on East 105$^{th}$ near Superior Avenue. They were also there when I got installed as pastor of Grace Tabernacle Baptist Church. Her husband did landscape work for free at our church, so I knew her heart, and I knew that when she said that word, she didn't know what she was saying, and it just slipped.

It's just like the "skin flute" incident, it slipped, and I didn't even know what it was. Me saying "skin flute" was the same as her saying "jigaboo." You've heard the word, but perhaps you don't know what it means. It all hit her so fast, and people came into the studio, and I was like, "Oh my gosh!"

People can be doggish. Somebody at our station put it on YouTube, and I believe the controversy would've died down quickly if it weren't for that. By the time she said "jigaboo," the Internet had grown up compared to when I said "skin flute" eight years earlier. That incident broke Kristi, and I saw her go through a lot of nonsense because of it. She almost lost her job because black folks were calling for her head.

She was made to go to several black churches, which she didn't mind doing, but the whole thing amounted to having to repent, and she did. I went with her a couple of times, but I believe that a lot of black folks had a problem with me standing up for her.

Some black folks in the community felt I should've been cold-blooded and dogmatic towards Kristi, but I knew she didn't mean it the way people thought she did.

Sometimes you must give grace when folks have given you grace, and I was given grace with the "skin flute" incident, so I felt she deserved that grace. I stood by her, knowing that's not who she is.

To her credit, Kristi put all that behind her, and she's come back from it well. Now, she's loved by the black community, and as a race, we're very forgiving. Last year, she was *Cleveland Magazine*'s most popular female anchor, and we must remember that people make mistakes.

She has no malice or prejudice in her body, and God bless her.

## Prayer Changes Things

Herb Thomas and I were sent down south by the station in the late 1990s to cover the burning of African-American churches. Horrible stories like that often prompted me to pray for the victims involved and for those of us that covered them.

Speaking of prayer, I noticed that the prayers brought unity to those at the station who participated, and this practice increased as my life began to transition to a more spiritual one. When I began studying and taking ministry classes, the Lord started working on my heart.

It was an incredible bonding experience, and it got to the point where me, Stefani, and meteorologist Andre Bernier prayed on the set before going on the air. Some people complained, and management told us to stop doing it, so we took our prayers to the lunchroom. That was many years ago, and I can't get anybody to do that now, but God bless Stefani and Andre for being a part of that.

Herb and I also covered the first black college football game in Northeast Ohio. It was the first time an HBCU (historically black colleges and universities) college football game was held in Cleveland. In preparation for that, Herb and I were sent to Hampton and Tuskegee universities.

What I remember most was a trip to Montgomery, Alabama, Herb's birthplace, to retrace the roots of my dear friend. During that assignment, we also visited the Edmund Pettus Bridge in Selma, where in 1965, the Reverend Dr. Martin Luther King Jr. and other demonstrators were brutally attacked for marching for civil rights. That day was a flashpoint in the Civil Rights Movement and became immortalized as Bloody Sunday. It was there that Herb and I knelt and prayed, thanking God for how far He had brought us as a race, and how he had blessed us in our individual lives.

To God be the glory.

## Takeaways from Chapter 8

### by Deante Young

Newscasters have a tough job. They are tasked with reporting humanity's ups and downs, which encompasses a limitless range of emotions. From joy and triumph to despair and disaster, they have seen it all, and I'm convinced the work sometimes takes its toll on them.

While reading Chapter 8, "In the Middle of History," I experienced emotional highs and lows as flashbacks went through my mind of the specific events that Wayne Dawson covered or experienced as a journalist. It's a wonderful occupation but it requires tons of emotional stamina to endure.

I was riveted as Dawson described his actions in the aftermath of the calamitous events of September 11, 2001. He went to a bookstore to grab uplifting reading material because of the stress and uncertainty of that day. I lived through it, but he covered it on live television, which to me is incredible.

I felt a renewed sense of pride as he described his own emotions on the historic date of November 4, 2008–the day that Barack Obama was elected the 44$^{th}$ U.S. President. It was the pinnacle of joyous occasions that involved large numbers of people.

I was reminded of the unprecedented strength that kidnapping victims Michelle Knight, Amanda Berry, and Gina DeJesus were forced to develop as they were tortured and held in captivity by the ultimate sicko for a decade. It also became apparent to me how blessed I am to not be any of those heavily victimized people.

I admire Wayne's capacity for self-awareness after the "skin flute" incident and forgiveness after the Kristi Capel gaffe. The delicate way he handled it all exemplified his humanity and Godliness.

Lastly, the prayer rituals he once held at the news station to uplift the spirit and morale of those who participated highlighted his tremendous leadership qualities. This chapter is an excellent reminder of why Wayne Dawson is a trusted journalist and a generational talent.

# Part III: An Objective Perspective

Wayne Dawson has made a career out of making a great first impression and following that up with a great "forever" impression. That said, this section is designed to highlight how the "seeds of greatness" is more than just a way to become great at a calling or a career.

They're also "seeds" within you that can help fill you with positive energy and great character, which will lead others to become better people and speak highly of you because of what you've brought to their lives.

What follows are 14 chapters from people I interviewed (myself included), who either know Wayne very well or who've been essential to his journey. Their interviews have been edited for clarity and grammar. In each instance, there is a fascinating anecdote, fact or experience that might surprise you—or make you emotional.

Grab a box of tissues and let's go!

-D.Y.

# Chapter 9

# Tammy Bishko
## Wayne's Eldest Daughter

My dad always talks about my birth being the line between him "hanging out and doing whatever" and "now I have a child, so I need to get myself together." He obviously chose to go to school, and my mom and I would drive to Kent and stay in his dorm. I have a picture from when I was two years old with my dad, and he had this big old afro. I remember those things the most because it was so impactful for me to be there with him while he was in school.

He wasn't like, "Oh my goodness, I have this baby here infringing upon my college experience." He always shares that story with the tone that I was *part* of that experience with him. And even though I don't remember any of it, the stories he tells about me being on campus or in his dorm always stand out. Unbeknownst to me, and maybe even to him at that point, it may have formed the beginning of our bond.

It might've also formed the beginning of my understanding that "No matter where you come from, your education is everything, and it can make or break whatever your future looks like." Hearing him talk about that experience with me really ingrained in my mind the importance of family and how a person can be inspired by their family. Education is important because, without that, it's really hard to make a way for yourself.

I can tell from conversations with my dad that my being at that dorm meant everything to him. He was twenty at the time, primetime for having a good time, but there he was with my mom and me.

He had a decision to make: he could party or make some life changes, and he chose to make changes. Our conversations about those years stand out to me because he's always in awe that I was a part of that journey.

When I was born, I lived with my mom in East Cleveland on Shaw Avenue because my dad was in school, and my granny lived right around the corner on Orinoco. My mom worked at the post office then, so we could only visit my dad on the weekends.

Even if I wasn't going to visit my dad, my mom's relationship with my granny was so tight that it never felt like a big gap in time that I didn't see him.

The family unit was very strong, and granny's house was like a second home for us. My granny was so present in my upbringing that I didn't feel Dad's absence. I was a big part of his core family, and my uncle and I grew up more like brother and sister than niece and uncle.

Even now, it's hard to refer to him as "uncle."

I shuffled around a lot of schools during my childhood, and by that time, my dad was a well-known public figure. I loved that more when I was younger because he would speak at various school functions whenever anything was going on at school.

He was always wonderful about things like that. When he was still a news reporter, my cousins would visit for the summer, and he would let us participate in news promos. You name it, and he was there.

The school faculty would say, "We're going to ask your dad to speak at graduation," or they would ask, "Can he come read to the students?" No matter what it was, it was always a no-brainer for him, and he made himself available.

My dad was so kind, and he would give autographs and shake hand after hand. It was so exciting for me, even though being so young, I didn't realize the magnitude of it.

I sometimes thought, "If he's *this* popular in Cleveland, I can't imagine what bigger stars go through." People would stop him in the grocery store to say, "Hi." It was exciting when I was younger, but as I got older, I was like, "C'mon, it's just my dad!"

There were times in public when I would think, "He didn't even buy me cookies the other day, and I'm mad at him. What do you mean you want to shake his hand in the grocery store?"

Throughout my life, I have witnessed his popularity grow in the Greater Cleveland area, and I can see that he genuinely has stayed the same in the way he greets people and is so approachable. As I got older, it went from being very exciting to me needing a break from the attention he was getting.

But in high school, it really began to click that he was important and did so much for the community, which made me appreciate it so much more once I became an adult.

Watching my kids grow up and seeing how their friends react to him is amazing, especially since their friends are 20 or 21 years old.

Much like my perception of him as a public figure evolved over time, so did our father/daughter relationship. Growing up, he was definitely "Dad," and I did not want to make him angry, so I followed the rules.

I was the only child for ten years, and a lot of responsibility came with that ten-year gap but respecting my parents was a no-brainer. My mom and dad were very much in sync about children being respectful and not talking back, which was ingrained in me from an early age.

During my "middle school to high school" years, I was trying to exert some level of independence, but Dad was still Dad, keeping the needle right on the vinyl.

To be clear, these weren't awful moments; it was just the reality that "these are the rules, and if you break them, there will be consequences."

Do I feel that, at times, he could've loosened the reins a little bit? Absolutely, but what child doesn't? I think during those times, we were the most out of sync because I was trying to grow up at 15 or 16 years old. I wanted certain freedoms, and he said, "No, this is my house, and these are the rules."

I don't remember many times when Dad had to raise his voice at me, but we had some tense moments, which I think is normal when a child starts to believe they can make their own decisions even though they still live with one of their parents.

As I got older and Mom and Dad split up, that changed our relationship because, honestly, I played both ends against the middle. If Mommy made me mad, I'd go stay with Daddy, and if Daddy made me mad, I'd go stay with Mommy. It wasn't until my college years at Cleveland State University that just me and my dad lived together.

This was right before he and LaVerne got married and my sister was still living with Mom. I was right around 21 years old.

We were father and daughter, but we were also roommates. He worked afternoons, and I was in school all day.

We were like two ships passing and what was remarkable about that time was we hung out and went to nightclubs together! He saw me as a friend, and I saw him as a friend, which completely changed our relationship.

I discovered another layer to him that I enjoyed, and that formed a friendship and the unexpected joy of having fun together.

It was one of the times in my life when I thought, "Dang, my dad is really cool!" and we really enjoyed each other. Then, of course, I graduated college, got married, and was caught up running my own life.

Five or six years into my marriage, Dad and I reconnected. We went to New York, our first trip since I was in college.

We had the best time, and I was able to connect with him in a way that didn't diminish my respect for him, but it showed me another layer of who he was as a person. That's not something that most of us get with our parents. He and I got along so well with each other, and we could go out to dance and have fun. Even now, we still travel together.

For years, our relationship has been great, and there's never been a rift that pulled us apart. We've been able to talk through any disagreements, but there haven't been many.

We've had a nice journey as father and daughter.

For his 50$^{th}$ birthday in 2005, LaVerne threw him a big party, and I had to give a speech. Although I'm a talker, I hate giving speeches. I remember telling him that night, "I get it now," because I didn't really understand why he was the way he was with me growing up until I became a mom.

It then made sense, whereas before, it felt unreasonable, and I thought, "I'm a good child. Why won't you let me do the things I want to do?"

Until I had kids, I didn't understand his need to hold on to his child as long as he could, and I don't think he could've communicated that to me at the time.

During my teenage years, he let my mom handle any situations with me and boys. When I went to prom, he kept the "dad" hat on and wasn't interested in friendly small talk. It was more like, "I'm Mr. Dawson." There weren't many boys around anyway.

I met my future husband in high school. Even though we're divorced now, he and my dad are still tight. But during those high school years, my dad kept the line very rigid, with no gray area for friendliness with guys I dated.

When Dad and LaVerne first got married, it was a difficult situation to navigate with mom. LaVerne tried really hard not to be a problem. She took my sister and me to lunch to connect, and I felt torn because I saw that my mother was upset. I also wanted to be there for her.

My sister was so young that she probably didn't understand everything. I was aware that the way I reacted and responded to Dad and LaVerne's marriage would be how my sister was going to react and respond.

I eventually had to remove myself from my mom's pain because I could no longer juggle everything going on with her, my dad, and me. Also, I was trying to establish a relationship with LaVerne—she has always been so caring and sweet to me.

There was no way that I could've been mean to her because she loved me just as my dad loved me. She helped plan my wedding and she made my dad happy, so I wasn't going to stand in the way of that. She made every effort to form a relationship with me and my sister, even accepting my kids as her own grandkids.

My Dad is such an important person in the Black community, which reminds me of a recent event that I attended with him. He was being honored with an award, and the presenter listed so many of Dad's accomplishments, and I was thinking, "Wow! That's my dad." He went from being a news reporter in the field being sent all over the place to a weekend anchor, and now a full-time weekday morning anchor. What is most impactful is that he shows the importance of longevity and loyalty because most people will leave a news station if they don't like what's going on.

My dad has been at the same station for practically my whole life.

Not many people can say that. There are so few African-American news reporters and anchors that it's hard to miss what he's been doing. It goes hand in hand with him being so approachable and willing to speak at events and organizations anytime someone asks, and he would have missed so many opportunities to connect if he had closed himself off. He is always willing to go the extra mile. If he hadn't been willing, he wouldn't have received so many accolades, which causes people to pay attention to what he says.

He never let being tired or feeling overwhelmed stop him from being available to people in his community. His impact became greater because he removed himself from in front of the camera in a studio and became a person. Being in the community and speaking at fashion shows or churches solidified his celebrity, not appearing daily on Fox 8.

His work in the community, including establishing The Dawson Foundation, supersedes anything he's ever done in front of the camera. Dad becoming a pastor is along the same lines because he was always going to churches and preaching, so when the opportunity presented itself at Grace Tabernacle, it was kind of natural for him, and it didn't surprise me.

He was already going from church-to-church speaking, so becoming a pastor at Grace just gave him a "home" to spread the word. The authenticity of his message comes from a certain nervousness because I believe it challenges his spirit.

My dad's ultimate legacy will be that of a man who grew up in the city, maintained his roots there, and took every opportunity possible to give back. He's been able to maintain a career and stay relevant through several management and societal changes, something not a lot of people can do.

His legacy will include his willingness to be approachable and a real person to others; it's hard to ignore that human side of a person. He's embraced that and allowed the community to embrace it. Everything he has done for the community will never be forgotten.

# Chapter 10

# Kristi Capel

*Fox 8 News in the Morning* co-anchor

The first time I met Wayne Dawson was during my initial interview at Fox 8. I was auditioning for the "weather" position, but I was still under contract at a different station.

Wayne Dawson, Kenny Crumpton, and Tracy McCool came to watch my tryout at the weather wall. Suddenly, Wayne came over and started playing Twister with me on the green wall. It became a joke, and everybody was laughing, and that was my interview!

A couple of hours later, I left, and I called my parents, telling them, "I don't know what just happened. I've never been to an interview like that." Two days later, Fox 8 called and said, "You got the job," and I was like, "What??!!"

I grew up in Kentucky and my dad is from Ohio, but we really didn't have much family here, so we rarely came back to Cleveland. About eight months after I was hired, I went back to doing the traffic because the other station wouldn't let me out of my contract.

From the first moment I met Wayne and the whole crew, I knew that it was something special to be on this show. The culture is so good that it never feels like work around here! After about a year of reporting the traffic, I got the anchor spot with Wayne.

Wayne and I have a special relationship because we've been able to share our faith all these years.

His family is like my family, and I didn't have that when I first came to Cleveland because mine is scattered across the country.

My parents came to Wayne's ordination to support him in becoming a pastor. My dad had the best time that day. They also attended a different church service where Wayne had spoken because they have always loved and supported him.

My mom passed away in December 2021, and Wayne surprised me by speaking at her funeral in Florence, Kentucky, where I grew up.

Wayne was a big part of whatever strength I managed to have while my mom was fighting cancer. We have a brother/sister relationship, and many people that watch our show send us tweets and emails telling us that our relationship is so much fun to watch because we're always laughing.

My nine-year-old picked up on it and suggested that we rename our show "Fox 8 Comedy Show," saying, "You guys are always laughing and having fun." We have the hard news, and it's tough, but when you're watching a morning show, there are times when you can have fun, laughing and drinking coffee while giving our meteorologist Scott Sabol a hard time—which is our favorite part of the morning.

We just have a blast.

I've been asked about Wayne's evolution since becoming a pastor, and honestly, he's always been a faith-filled guy. In the twelve years I've been here, we've shared our faith, and now I think it's grown.

I wouldn't say he's a different person, but I think his relationship with God is at a higher level. He was already a great witness and example, and God has given him a platform by being on this show.

I also think God has given him another platform to add to what he's doing on TV, which is really cool, and the station backs him when his church is handing out food or sponsoring special events.

He's at a whole 'nother level with his relationship and is doing a fantastic job, and the church adores him. He's broadening his horizons in the church with the children's church. Little by little, he chips away at different ideas and continues to build the church and make it better than it was.

God knew what He was doing when He put these platforms in Wayne's life. He's always been a great guy, but now he's even better. He and his wife LaVerne are a classy, Godly example for the city.

Wayne is also very loyal, which translates to friendship, and others can always count on him. People in the media can be different off the set sometimes than when they're on TV. When Wayne and I are attending or emceeing station events, I always hear people commenting that he is the same off camera as he is on camera.

His friendship and loyalty are no different than how we interact on the show. He's always been a good friend and I speak very highly of his family because you can see how he's raised his kids, too.

He's an awesome dad and grandpa, a loyal friend you can talk to or share anything with, and you can see that reflects in his family. He's just an awesome all-around guy.

NOTE: *In February 2015, during a Fox 8 News in the Morning episode, Kristi unknowingly said a racial slur twice on the air while commenting on a segment of the Academy Awards to Wayne. The situation became national news and brought a lot of negative attention to Kristi.*

I don't like to talk about that incident, but how Wayne handled it is a great example of his loyalty. As I've said before, it was something I wasn't aware of and got educated quickly. People who didn't really know me came up with their own opinions. I'm frequently asked about it, and what I can say for sure is that Wayne had my back the whole time.

He believed me and therefore was able to tell people that I really am an awesome person. I was very grateful to him for that.

Wayne does so much to help others. He's always looking for opportunities, especially with the Dawson Foundation, to bless so many kids.

It's great that he and his brother have been doing that for so long in their mother's name, and I know she would be extremely proud of them.

Wayne is always looking for opportunities to make a difference in people's lives, whether speaking at schools or raising money for something. He and I have been hosting the March of Dimes and a few other things for the past ten or eleven years. Honestly, I wonder if he ever sleeps! He's constantly in the community trying to make a difference, and I have always looked up to him for that, especially when I first got here. He's helped me build relationships with people so that I could also help in the community.

Wayne has given me so much good advice over the years, and I think that my favorite is when he told me to be myself and have fun when I first got on the show.

At the time, Tracy McCool was doing mornings, and those were some big shoes to fill. When she moved to evenings, I was promoted to the morning show with Wayne. He just said, "We have a lot of fun on this show, and we're on the air longer than anybody else in town. It's going to be a long morning, but just have fun, and people will love you!"

He's been so great for so long that he will always be remembered for the good that he's done. His legacy here in Cleveland will be the sacrifices he made in giving to the community.

Wayne has been winning people over to the Lord, which is most important. He's a fabulous co-worker and anybody that you talk to would agree with that!

# Chapter 11

# LaVerne Dawson
### Wayne's Wife of 25 years and
### the First Lady of Grace Tabernacle

The first time I saw Wayne Dawson in person was in 1983. I met with my mom's dear friend, Mrs. Bernice Edwards in downtown Cleveland for lunch that day. She was a trailblazer in business and a wonderful mentor who would later inspire me to open my beauty salon.

As she and I were walking and talking, I felt a set of eyes on me and lo and behold, it was Mr. Dawson; the reporter from *Newscenter 8* doing a "stand-up" on an historical building being demolished on Public Square in downtown Cleveland.

That's my story and I'm sticking to it.

But seriously, I'm not sure but it *seemed* like we caught each other's eyes.

Fast forward to 1987, which was about a year after I opened my beauty salon in Cleveland Heights. I was a 26-year-old innovative entrepreneur, working day and night to build my brand. I was also the new kid on the block working ten to twelve hours a day and it all began with that dear friend of my mom's, Mrs. Edwards.

It had been four years since I last saw Wayne in person, but that changed one evening at a jazz club called "The Reason Why" in Shaker Square. They were holding a panel discussion consisting of young professionals about relationships. A nurse, who was also one of my hair clients had invited me and another girlfriend whom I worked with, to attend.

After the forum, the club opened the dance floor.

Sitting, chatting and having fun with the girls, I noticed this cool, smooth, handsome and collected TV reporter coming in with another fine brother that my girlfriend noticed. That young and bold version of myself got up from my seat and formally introduced myself to Wayne Dawson. Soon, we danced, then sat and talked.

I found him to be sweet, kind, and down to earth and after that night, we casually kept in touch. With him being a fairly new reporter and me being a new business owner, we both were focused on our crafts. Periodically, we would run into each other at some of the same events.

Ironically, we knew some of the same people– the eminent Dr. Yvonne Pointer being one, and she remains a close friend today. She was also influential in Wayne and I getting together.

What drew me to Wayne initially was a few things. First, I thought he was very handsome, and I felt like I knew him from seeing him on television. After dancing and talking with him at "The Reason Why," I discovered his charm, intelligence, compassion and warm heart. I soon realized "the reason why" our paths crossed: our lives were predestined.

Honestly, he had me at "Hello."

I always believed that we had the potential to have more than just a causal relationship. I wasn't really dating much at the time (a blind date here and there). Instead, I was working from sunup to sundown to build a new business. When Wayne became single and available, I was also single, available and still working day and night.

Wayne was different from the kind of men I had dated as a youngster. I was an inner-city girl who had gotten caught up with the bad boys, but I knew early on they weren't my type, and whom I wanted a future with.

As I said early on, when I met Wayne, he had me at "hello," so it was easy to envision life with him.

That's not to say I knew he was the one, or if it would've happened, because our lifestyles were as far apart as the east is to the west. His time, availability and interest were elsewhere, and I was totally married to my business.

Wayne was 41 when he lost his mother and had recently broken up with his longtime girlfriend and the mother of his children. When I heard about the passing of his mother, I really wanted to be there for him. I didn't go to her funeral, but I did offer to take care of providing food for the repast.

I believe at that point we reconnected, and he probably saw me in a different light. He began to evolve after the death of his mother and began to build a closer connection with God. We began a more serious relationship after he lost his mom and got married a year later, on August 29, 1997.

When Wayne and I got married, an evolution had to take place and we had to grow into being a couple. No more "this is mine and this is yours." In marriage, you grow and evolve into it, it doesn't happen overnight.

It was somewhat of a Cinderella story and somewhat not. I moved in after we got back from our honeymoon. Our life together began and not without its ups and downs. Early in our relationship, I dealt with a lot of insecurities. I didn't know how to handle his celebrity status, which caused issues in our marriage. But I thank God for my husband's patience and the love he has for me. He reminds me of the vows we made to one another, and they cannot be easily broken.

I feel that I am the most blessed woman to have found the love of my life. It doesn't mean that we don't have disagreements and sometimes strong disagreements. But to God be the glory, we just celebrated 25 years of marriage, and we're still going strong and looking forward to the next phase of what God has in store for us.

There are many things I love about my husband. He is a "girl dad"(to three young women) and I always admired how much he loves his girls. He never put anything or anyone before them. With all of my insecurities and hang ups, questioning Wayne's love for his daughters wasn't one of them.

In those early years, it was most admirable to see him as a hands-on, doting dad with Tammy and Crystal. I thought about how lucky I would be to marry a man like that, and lo and behold, he's that same doting dad with Danielle, our youngest daughter.

If anyone sees me as being a good wife, it's because God has blessed me with a good husband, who's come into my life and helped me become the person I am today. Whatever he has said I've brought into his life, he has more than equaled that in mine.

My husband's legacy will consist of many things: being a man who loves the Lord and his family, his professionalism, he's favored by people from many walks of life, the launch of the Annie L. Dawson Foundation, his longevity at Channel 8, his love for Cleveland's sports teams (the Browns, Guardians and Cavaliers), his generosity in how he gives his time and talents to a city he loves, and last but not least, he is an awesome and loving pastor.

# Chapter 12

# William Dawson –
## Wayne's Brother and East Cleveland Judge

Wayne grew up in a home with our mother, father, and grand-mother. By the time I was a toddler, my father had left, so my mother was solely responsible for my upbringing, and she put demands on Wayne to stay out of trouble and be successful.

My memory is very choppy up until Wayne's college years when he would come home on the weekends. I remember Wayne being enrolled in the media program in college, and by the time I was in elementary school, Wayne was on TV. I've always been very proud of my brother, and I knew what he was doing was extraordinary, considering the rarity of anyone being on television.

Wayne was more of a father figure than a brother to me, so I wasn't really inspired by his achievements because, knowing that he was my older brother, he also had expectations of me. That meant if my mother didn't catch me being a knucklehead, he surely would have, so my thinking was "I better not mess up," which helped me not be starstruck by him. Kids at my school would always say, "Oh my God, your brother is Wayne Dawson!"

My feelings about that were, "Yeah, that's my brother, but he's on my butt all the time."

That kept me grounded, and it's helped me my entire life because I've been able to establish a relationship with Wayne that is not based on his celebrity. It's based on respect for him as a person, father figure, and mentor in my life.

One thing that *has* been inspiring to me about Wayne is his evolution as a man. He's always had a heart full of love and the spirit to give back and help others. His growth since he and LaVerne entered marriage has been great to see. He went from being what many of us can honestly say was a classic example of a young man who grew up in the ghetto with ghetto morals.

Those tend to revolve around things we can control, so we want possessions and women, and many of us get caught up in that. Many years ago, he dated different women and wasn't committed as he is now. He's married and fully committed to being a man of God and having a Godly marriage.

There was a time when if someone asked if my brother would ever get married, I would've probably said, "No." Some people you can see them being married in the future, but with Wayne, I never saw it coming because that wasn't necessarily what was important to him. His career, family, and giving back were important to him, but being in a single relationship was not at the time.

LaVerne hijacked his mentality, which happens with many men. When you find the right woman, they come in and blow up everything you thought you were on the path to do. She took Wayne from where he was as a single man and molded him into a marriageable man and a husband.

On the other hand, when my brother decided to become a pastor, it didn't surprise me. Even before Wayne became a married man, the direction of his heart was always pointing him to be a Godly man.

Since I have been so close to him for many years, I saw it long before he became a pastor. If you have an important relationship with the Lord and you are a natural motivator and have a heart for people, those things often connect so, it was no surprise to me.

Creating the Dawson Foundation with Wayne was a natural step to take, notwithstanding anything he's done in the community. Because of the deep love and respect that we both have for our mom and what she taught us, it was a no-brainer to use that opportunity to give back to others.

We knew that the way our mother raised us meant there was more we could do together to honor her legacy and what she taught us.

I've heard people refer to Wayne as a powerful and important figure for us, and I happen to agree, especially because he's on TV and continues to be a voice of reason. Still, I think he possesses one very important quality that no one else has zeroed in on: the power of a black man being consistent.

Wayne has done the morning show for 23 years and counting, and how many times have we turned on the TV and Wayne wasn't on-set because he was late?

Zero.

Wayne has never been late to work. He has called in sick when he didn't feel well, but his consistency in showing up as a professional black man is something we overlook.

One thing we can count on in the morning is turning on the TV and seeing what Wayne Dawson is wearing or what he's talking about because he's not going to let us down. We've become so used to that as a community that some of us think it's not a big deal, but it is a big deal because young people need to know the value of consistency and reliability.

He shows those qualities every day, even when he's not talking about it. If you open your eyes, you will see it—he's there every day doing the news professionally and giving it his best. No matter what is going on in his life, at home, or at the church, we only see professionalism and consistency which should be taught in schools.

Young people need to be consistent and reliable and not allow their emotions and other distractions to take away from what they are doing with their lives. Leadership by example is one of the hidden powers of Wayne Dawson that often goes unnoticed, but it's important.

Those are all elements of Wayne's ultimate legacy, but there's so much more to it. He is an amazing professional and an example of excellence. Young people who decide to go into the television industry can look to Wayne Dawson and see his professionalism, hard work, and dedication. He is a great example of what it takes to be a reporter and newsman. We have gotten so comfortable with technology and having access that we have dumbed down so many things, even news.

No longer are people like Wayne required to stand in front of a mirror and practice speaking for hours. As a young man, I witnessed him repeatedly read quotes that were written on his mirror while he was putting on his tie or brushing his teeth to empower and encourage himself and ensure he could enunciate words in a way that everyone could understand him.

Now, anyone can get on the radio or a television show while sounding as if they don't have a high school diploma. Anyone wanting to know what it takes to be a newscaster can Google and review Wayne Dawson's news clips, and that will be a blueprint. His legacy in the profession is undeniable. He's up there with Walter Cronkite and all the current national guys in terms of professionalism.

Another part of his legacy is his consistency in being a man of God and a positive person in our community. He has stood the test of time by being someone who it can be said is a good man or brother. The saying goes that if you last long enough, your heroes turn into villains, but that hasn't happened to Wayne, and it's a beautiful thing.

He didn't have to go into the ministry to do what he does now. Most of our long-lived heroes are ministers because when they make it to sixty, seventy, or eighty years old, they're not doing crazy stuff anyway. At this point, Wayne motivates me to keep the legacy of the Dawson name going, and I do not undervalue what he has done for our last name.

I was an attorney before I became a judge, and I was seen as *just* an attorney. But when I was Attorney Dawson running for judge, I was Wayne's brother so, his good name carried a lot of weight for me. I acknowledge that and won't deny it because I know what he's built for me.

I always tell people in my courtroom that their name matters, and it's going to matter to their kids. I use my situation with Wayne as an example, and I explain that they will want their kids to stand in front of somebody and be asked, "What's your name? Oh, I knew your father or your mother." Instead, many of us are damaging our legacy so early that people look down on us, and it transfers to our children when they grow up and mention their last name.

I proudly tell my children that they are Dawsons, and their name stands for integrity, consistency, and hard work. Of course, my kids are in elementary school currently, so it's hard to get them to understand that, but I still want them to hear it.

# Chapter 13

# Virgil Dominic
## Former Channel 8 News Director Who Hired Wayne

After graduating from Kent State University, Wayne came to see me. He brought some of his writings and videotapes for me to review, and we began a conversation. He was obviously very talented, and I could see his potential right off the bat. By the time I met Wayne, I had been a reporter, an anchorman, and a network correspondent for many years. When you have that experience, you can get a feeling right away as to whether a potential reporter has that innate ability to become a really good reporter.

I remember that Wayne was very eager. He really wanted to be in the business and make it his life. Sometimes through experience, you meet some people who think they want to be reporters because it appears glamorous. So, I questioned Wayne along those lines, and he had no interest in that whatsoever. He didn't see it as something entertaining; he wanted to be a serious journalist, which is exactly what I was looking for as the news director.

I then asked him how he felt about additional training because Kent State is a wonderful university, and I admire the journalism department so much. But there's an inevitable transition that one must go through when getting to a professional station in a highly competitive market.

At that time, Channel 8 was in third place out of three news stations, so it was incumbent upon me as the news director to find just the right kind of people willing to be trained. I had not set out in my career to become a news director, but through the hand of God, I ended up going to Atlanta, where I became a news director for the first time.

I figured the only way to improve the station was to improve the quality of people. In my humble judgment, that meant I had to teach them what I had learned from my mentors, and the only way to do that was to work individually with the reporters and the camera people.

I became a "teaching" news director, and that worked. Within three years, this poor third-place station became number one and knocked off a station in Atlanta that had been number one for 50 straight years.

We changed Atlanta television forever. So, when I came back to Cleveland, a third-place station, it was important for me to determine whether people wanted to be trained. Some people think they know it all because they've graduated from college, but "eager" was the word for Wayne.

He easily accepted the fact that he needed to know more, so I hired him on the spot. I was impressed with him for several reasons, but there is something else in the hiring process for television news that I've learned, and I firmly believe.

The goodness in a person.

Somehow, the audience could tell, and it was obvious to me, that Wayne was a very good person with good morals. He had an absolute commitment to helping others and being kind. I sensed that in him, and that really pushed me into hiring him.

When we started working together, I was trying to assemble a really good team of good people and run a news department that clearly needed to do something different.

The staff was not disciplined, so I worked with everyone I hired individually, and I would call Wayne because I wanted to teach him what I believed was the clear and best definition of news. I asked him, "What is 'news'?" He described it to me, and he was right, but then I told him the difference in what *our* newscast was going to be.

"The definition of 'news' for Channel 8 is now 'something that is interesting, and if it's not interesting, it cannot be news because nobody will watch it, listen to it or read it,'" I said to Wayne. I went on to say, "You can come to me and say, 'This story has got to go on the air because it's important,' and I will say to you, 'It's not going to get on the air, but I have enough confidence in you that if it's important, you will figure out a way to make it interesting.'"

In the early days of Wayne's training, I would call him every morning and assign news story ideas to him and get his opinion on how to do the story and what approach to take.

"Who would you interview?"

"What places would you visit?

"What visuals would you use?"

After he did the story, we would watch it together so I could offer my critique:

"Wayne, this part of the story was good," I'd say, and then I would tell him *why* it was good.

Never in my career as a news director have I ever told anybody that they made a mistake. I would simply review a story and inquire if they had asked a different question in their interview, would it have made it better? That is how I taught reporters how to do interviews and make them interesting.

After much practice, Wayne kept getting better and better in all aspects; reporting, writing, and anchoring, and then came the transition: I no longer had to give him stories because he brought his own to me. From there, he continued to grow and grow.

It's important to remember that during the early days of Wayne's career, Channel 8 was in third place, and I was looking for anything to make the newscast better. Hiring the right people and having the right ideas is the only way to accomplish that. So, at midnight every night, Channel 8 would run a spiritual one-or two-minute feature by Sister Juanita Sheeley, a wonderful nun who became the patron saint of Channel 8.

The feature that I watched each day was beautifully produced, well photographed, and edited. I was told that a man named Herb Thomas, who worked in our carpentry shop and put together our sets was responsible for that.

I found Herb and asked, "Herb, have you ever thought about becoming a news photographer?"

He said he'd never thought about it, but soon, I was training Herb to become just that—our news photographer and a producer. This moment was very important for the trajectory of Wayne Dawson's career because I ultimately linked Herb and Wayne together as a team.

By that point, Wayne had developed a real insight into what a story should be, and he began realizing that there were stories we were doing and stories we were *not* doing. One day, he came to me with an idea; a lot of positive stories were happening in the African-American communities of Cleveland, but nobody knew about them. Wayne proposed that we start doing stories on those individuals who were making a positive difference.

It was a great idea, so I suggested that we do a monthly series—a 30-minute program—and that's exactly what we did. It was the first time in

Cleveland television history that an entire program had been devoted to African- Americans doing good and major service in the community.

The Herb Thomas/Wayne Dawson team became widely recognized in the community and won several Emmy awards. They were a terrific team, and their partnership became a major catapult for Wayne to become well-known in the community. This eventually led to the anchorman position at Channel 8. He got better and better at it, and now he's been an anchorman for a number one show for close to a quarter-century.

What still comes through in Wayne's anchoring to this day is not only his journalistic abilities but also his goodness. He has an innate sense of service that endears him to the community. He volunteers a lot of time and does work that helps people and organizations. He receives no money for it, which is unusual for anyone, but Wayne does things out of the kindness of his heart, and I think that led him to become a pastor.

Serving people has always been of utmost importance to Wayne Dawson, and that's part of the goodness I saw in him the first time I interviewed him. Part of his legacy will be that of a beloved anchorman for more years than any other anchorman in the history of Cleveland television.

His legacy will be that of a man who embodied the utmost professionalism, dedication to the job, service to the community, and devotion to the care of others.

# Chapter 14

# Melva Hadley
### Wayne's Oldest Living Relative

Wayne is my cousin—my mother was Wayne's mother's sister. I didn't see Wayne becoming a broadcaster when he was young, but as he got a little older, he told me he wanted to be a sports commentator. He was into sports, and I was really surprised that he didn't go into that field. I know if his mom were still alive, she'd be so proud of him and William.

I spent a lot of time around Wayne when he was young, but I wasn't around him much until after he graduated from high school. His mom and I would talk about him often.

He's always been very intelligent, a good kid, and down-to-earth, and his attitude hasn't changed. A lot of people in my apartment building tease me and say, "You're only watching Channel 8 because Wayne's on there," and I tell them that I've watched Channel 8 since I was five or six years old.

I'm blessed to have him as a family member.

I was really happy for Wayne when he first appeared on television, and I thought to myself, "My goodness, he's come a long way." I used to watch him in the field when he was still a reporter. A couple of times, he took me out with him.

I was even happier when they made him an anchor. He's been on TV a long time, and I tease him sometimes that he's going to be Dick Goddard all over again.

Wayne said he's going to try to do a few more years and then retire. We'll see… he enjoys what he's doing and likes to keep busy.

Now that he is a pastor, I tell him to take care of his health because he's doing so much and getting older. Soon, he's going to catch up with me, and I'm 80 years old.

I really liked LaVerne when I met her and was happy when she and Wayne got married. She is a blessing to him.

When he was close to becoming a pastor, I went to his event at Bethany Baptist Church and thought, "Wow! My Wayne," when I heard him preach.

I was so outdone by him and didn't know he could sing like he did. I'm glad that he's come such a long way with his life. Although I was surprised he became a pastor at first, I remember when he was young that his mother never missed a night getting down on her knees in prayer. Sometimes she would be down there for so long that I wondered if she fell asleep.

Wayne was raised very well by his mom, and I feel that he was chosen spiritually, which helped him get as far as he has. He is very important to the city of Cleveland. For those who don't know him and only see him on TV, I let them know that he's still down to earth and the same as he was when he was growing up.

People talk about legacy, but my memory of Wayne will be of everything that he's done for me. He makes me feel like I come first, has never let me down, and helped me in many ways. He's blessed, has his calling, God is on his side, and whatever He wants Wayne to do, it will get done.

Wayne really helped me after my dad died. He prayed with me and inspired me. Sometimes, I call him and ask him to speak the word to me, and he does. He and LaVerne have loving spirits, and I really appreciate that from them. I've been blessed just to have him in my life and family, and I know that I can call if I need him.

# Chapter 15

# Yvonne Pointer
## Community Activist

On December 6, 1984, my daughter Gloria Pointer was brutally raped and murdered. Wayne Dawson and I made eye contact for the first time when I was coming out of her funeral.

There was a barrage of media there, but Wayne stood out, and he became my go-to person when I needed media coverage for families victimized by violence. I could call Wayne, and he would put me in contact with families and allow me to get help for them.

My daughter's homicide wasn't solved for 29 years. Wayne would always invite me as a guest on Fox 8 to help me promote what I was doing on my journey to find her killer. I could always count on Wayne Dawson and Fox 8 to give me a media platform.

As I said, there were a lot of news reporters in the city, but I think that Wayne and I connected because he's one of us. He's an East Cleveland boy, and he's not highfalutin. Some people are unapproachable and untouchable, but Wayne has always represented the African-American community as a *member* of the African-American community.

I connected him and his wife LaVerne. She and I were good friends, and she expressed an interest in getting to meet Wayne. We sent Wayne Dawson some flowers from her, and that was the start of their connection.

LaVerne's mom and I were raised in the same church, so I would see her because she was also brought up in the church. That's how I got to be their daughter's godmother.

Over the years, I was involved with *Parents of Murdered Children, Parents Against Child Killing, Positive Plus* (to support women), and now *The Hope Haven*, a Facebook show that I do Monday through Friday that reaches people around the world.

When we started building schools in Africa in memory of my daughter, Wayne was always my go-to person, and I could always count on being a guest on Fox 8. I called Ed Gallek when the news broke that my daughter's killer had been arrested; he worked with me on the street level.

Wayne is approachable, compassionate, and a kind soul. He's a remnant of his mother who never forgot where he came from. I remember when I received the Essence award in New York, and Steve Harvey was in the lobby. I walked over to him and said, "Hi Mr. Harvey, I'm from Cleveland," and he looked at me like I was yesterday's boo-boo on a dirt farm!

In my mind, he could've said, "Hello," but that's something that would never come from Wayne. I feel that I'm just like him because we are ordinary people whom God has called to do extraordinary things.

I don't think Wayne gets the credit he deserves because the anchors on Fox 8 are not representative of our community. I'm thankful that Wayne has been there for so long because we need him.

# Chapter 16

# LaRese Purnell
## Managing Partner of Cleveland Consulting Firm

I met Wayne when I was working as the chief of staff at the Word Church, and he would come to do interviews with Pastor Vernon. We got to know each other, and he was very supportive of the work we were doing in the community. I naturally took a liking to him and had a lot of respect for the way he carried himself.

Wayne is what his brother would call a cycle-breaker and a trendsetter because his day-to-day actions make him very relatable, and he's also very transparent and supportive.

He knows who he is as an individual, and I think that's important because people can have a role but lose themselves in it. When you're talking to Wayne, you're not talking to Wayne the personality or the celebrity; it's always him, and he's always being his true self.

That's important and allows him to build relationships. In this community, if you're going to tell your story, you want Wayne to tell it for you. He will be protective of your story and ask the right questions. Even the way he looks when he's on TV, he is a trendsetter and is a standard in our community in and out of his industry.

He's a family man, and whenever I run into him and LaVerne with their children, it drives that point home. He's also a Christian man, so I get the best of both worlds from Wayne, the real world and the spiritual world. He has a great reputation, values his name, and has created a legacy in which the Dawson name means something in this community.

Wayne is also a man of his word. If he tells you that he's going to do something, he does it. He inspires me in the way that he lights up a room when he's in it, and he encourages me to engage others because he's all about bringing people together and loving them. He loves speaking life into people, which is why I love being around him because he greets you with inspiring words and leaves you with inspiring words, and it's never about him.

He is attentive and prepared, and in a community full of issues, Wayne is a breath of fresh air, and he's someone who can be counted on because he's both a role model and a roadmap for so many people. You never know that you're making history when you're in it, but Wayne is someone we'll talk about when he's long gone, which is encouraging to me as a black man in this community.

Wayne is vital to everything that he touches. In the world of broadcasters, he is an icon. In the religious community, he's an icon. In terms of community impact and outreach, he's an icon. When we talk about being a family man, he's an icon. So, in every area that he's involved in, he's an iconic standard, and you will hear the same type of things about him from people who've met him: "Wayne's a great guy!"

In our community, many black men are in prison or living in poverty. Wayne is an iconic figure to people of all age groups and all communities, and of course, we want to take credit for him because he is a black man, but people respect him no matter what their background is.

During the pandemic, I watched Wayne's sermons online, and it became clear to me that TV was just one platform of many. He's going to be himself no matter where he's at. It's no different than if he was talking onstage at Playhouse Square versus talking at Fox 8 versus church–Wayne is Wayne. If you know him and see him in different situations, you will see the consistency. But you'll also see that preaching the word is a real passion and calling for him, and it's just another avenue to continue doing more things in the community.

Before Wayne got his own church, I always saw him as a spiritual guy because he would always say things like "God bless you" and "I'm praying for you," depending on whatever I was doing at the time.

Wayne's legacy will be that he was the voice of the community. People remember him setting the table for our community and giving access to so many people. When he tells their story, he opens the door and changes careers, families, attitudes, culture, and so much more by being and doing what he does. It's easy to see that God uses him as a conduit in that role. Wayne told my story years ago, and people started saying, "Who is this guy that Wayne's talking to?"

When he gives you access to the table, then Channels 3, 5, and 19 call you. Everybody else calls you because, again, he is the standard. When you are the standard, and you give people access to you, then you give them access to everything that exists within your atmosphere. He will be known for giving people access and for his community impact.

Wayne's foundation provides resources and he is always ready to show up for your event and bring light to it. He's a community activist in a sense and being in that role, he provides opportunities for people. I know they will be forever grateful for his willingness to do that.

It's easy for people to be in a role and do things that are expected of them, but Wayne has allowed others in his industry who look like him to follow his lead and make sure everybody has a voice.

# Chapter 17

# Rev. Dr. Stephen Rowan

Senior Pastor at Bethany Baptist Church
in Cleveland and Spiritual Mentor to Wayne

Wayne Dawson attended Bethany as a boy. He would come with his grandparents, whom I remember fondly as very nice people. He really grew up in the church under my dad, Dr. A.T. Rowan, the pastor at Bethany for 35 years. After going away to school, Wayne came back and continued to be at Bethany.

I later became the pastor, succeeding my dad. Then Wayne accepted his call to the ministry, and I was privileged to ordain him. He served under my leadership for some years before he was called to Grace Tabernacle.

Pastor Pryce of Grace Tabernacle called me when he was ill, and I became the pastor for him and his wife, Juliet, as he was in and out of the hospital. As his illness progressed, he talked about his transition and succession plan and his thoughts for the church. Then, he asked me about Wayne.

Pastor Pryce made it known that he was interested in Wayne as a possible successor to him at Grace Tabernacle.

I arranged a meeting with Wayne and Pastor Pryce before Grace Tabernacle called Wayne up as the pastor. It was a great opportunity for Wayne, although I don't think he was "looking to pastor."

I spent a lot of time with Wayne at Bethany, frequently during sick visits. He and I would visit members in nursing homes and hospitals, so I had many chances to talk with him.

I heard about his hopes for the ministry, and as he grew in it and went to seminary, I tried to mentor him as best I could. He was always a very willing mentee and is a good man who cares about people and loves the Lord, so he had many of the attributes that you look for in a pastor—not just a preacher because pastoring is completely different from preaching.

Pastoring is a 24/7 job, and I felt that Wayne has a heart for the people, so I'm not surprised that he became a pastor.

When we would be in public, it was most obvious. I didn't really know how he would be when he told me that he felt a call on his life, but I've watched him; he's very good with people, which is a requirement in this line of work.

He wants to do the right thing, serve the Lord, and please God, even though the Bible tells us it's impossible to please God because we're sinners born into sin, and we have our flaws, faults, and failures. I'm not saying that Wayne is perfect, and certainly, I know I'm not perfect. But I do know that when it comes to trying to please the Lord, that's what he's doing.

A couple of things stand out in my mind when looking back on Wayne's installation service in 2018. First, it was standing room only! We must remember that a lot of people know who he is, and they like him. There was a lot of enthusiasm, and you could feel the presence of the Holy Spirit.

It was an exciting and joyful day, and people were happy to be there and see Wayne become a pastor. I was happy as well, but I had warned him to understand what he was getting himself into if he did this. He told me that he felt it was what God wanted him to do, and from then on, I've been supportive.

I observed how he handled people and, of course, everywhere we'd go, people would say, "Oh, Mr. Dawson!" and other times, "Leon Bibb!!!" I was tickled about that, but he was always very calm and very polite to people, often taking selfies with them. He was unruffled and very humble about it, and we would just keep on moving.

I've always found him to have a humble spirit in moving about with him, and he's never been disrespectful towards me as the pastor.

I believe that pastoring has not only made Wayne a better man, but it also taught him discipline. The Bible says the fear of God is the beginning of wisdom, and the Bible says to work out your salvation with fear and trembling. It doesn't mean the worldly type of fear, but it means to do it with a healthy respect for God. Wayne has that healthy respect for who God is, and who God is to him and in his life and the impact that God has had on his life.

I tell our people and myself, "We're here by the grace of God." We see things happen to innocent people, but we're saved by the grace of God. I think Wayne realizes that he's in God's protective custody, which he appreciates and has made an impact.

In my opinion, Wayne's ultimate legacy will be that he had staying power. To be at one television station that long, mentoring many people, was a role model for youth, a good family man, cared about the community, and he certainly loved the Lord. People don't care how much you know until they know how much you care...and he cares.

He's a sensitive guy in many ways that people don't understand and he's very reflective. He pays attention to what goes on around him and he's very astute about things.

His legacy will also be one of someone who was bi-vocational, and he did it well, putting his best foot forward and giving it all he possibly could with the help of the Lord.

# Chapter 18

# Stefani Schaefer

Co-anchor of *Fox 8 News in the Morning*
and Wayne's Friend for 30 years

I met Wayne Dawson on my first day at Fox 8 in August 1992. We've had such a great rapport with each other from the very beginning. To sum it up perfectly, Wayne and I would take bullets for each other, and from the minute we met, we were always on the same page.

He had been in the business for over ten years by the time I got to Channel 8, and even though he was seasoned, he didn't act like one of those "hard" journalists. Of course, he was experienced, but he was still very sweet, and I was just trying to feel my way through this.

I had just graduated and had grown up in the small town of Alliance, so Cleveland was still like "the big city" to me. Then suddenly, I was working in this industry.

I remember having a really bad day because some of these stories were getting to me. I'm very emotional anyway, but this stuff can affect anyone.

I covered some emotional stories about kids being injured or killed in car accidents. I would think, "Oh my gosh, this is so depressing. This is so hard," and "Maybe I'm not in the right field." I felt like maybe I shouldn't be there, and Wayne said to me: "Sissy, you got to wear a raincoat and let it just slide off your back. When you walk out the door, you can't carry this with you because you're too emotional."

That was great advice coming from such a well-respected human being. When he said that to me, it was like our first brother/sister moment. I cried in his arms, and he was like, "You're going to be okay," and "It's alright. We got to toughen you up a little bit."

I would share my story with other people, and they would say, "Oh, put on a happy face," or "You'll be fine, hang in there." But when Wayne said that stuff to me, I knew he meant it. He would check on me and help guide me. Then, we started working weekends together, became co-anchors, and we've been like brothers and sisters. We always say that we know everything about each other.

When we were both single and finding our way in Cleveland, we would share stories. I'd be like, "What do you think of this guy?" He'd give me the truth and say, "I don't like him" or "I like him," which was cute because he was that big brother to me. I knew he had my back, loved me, respected me, and picked me up. You can't find a lot of people who you can truly trust, and from day one, I trusted Wayne, and he has always been a devoted friend.

When Wayne started dating LaVerne, and I started dating Roger, the four of us would do things together as couples. Roger and I got married soon after Wayne and LaVerne. We had a son, Race. 18 months later, their daughter Danielle was born, and she is two months older than my daughter Siena.

We did a lot of things together as a family: birthday parties, christenings, et cetera. Our relationship has truly stood the test of time and has evolved.

When I was working and living in Orlando, he and his family came to visit us. It's a special relationship that goes way beyond a "work" relationship. Wayne has always been more of a brother to me than a co-worker, and during the darkest days of my life, he stood right by my side.

Wayne and I would pray for the victims in the stories we would report every day before a newscast.

On April 27, 2012, Wayne and I had just finished the morning show, and I got the call in the newsroom from Roger's boss, Rob, telling me that Roger had fallen twelve feet off scaffolding and was being rushed to Hillcrest Hospital.

I could tell from Rob that it wasn't good. I was in the newsroom filled with people, saying things like, "Oh dear God." My news director at the time, Sonya Thompson, could hear me asking, "What hospital?" and saying, "I'll be there right now!"

I kicked off my high heels and started running down the hallway barefoot. Wayne had already left the station, so Sonya called him and said, "Get to Hillcrest Hospital. Something's going on with Sissy and Roger."

The minute I got to Hillcrest, I was ushered into a private room with a couch, table, chair, and a box of tissues. Because they didn't let me stay in the emergency room, I knew the news was grim. Wayne walked in just as the doctor said they were getting Roger ready for Life Flight to Metro Hospital. I looked at Wayne and said, "You know what that means!"

Wayne and I had done numerous news stories over the years, and we knew that Metro was the only Level I trauma center nearby. As news people, we knew some things that others may not have known. Either the situation was as bad as it could be for an accident, or it could mean they were going to harvest organs for donation.

Wayne hugged me and we cried and prayed together. Roger's mom came to the hospital, and she, Wayne, and I got to see Roger. He couldn't talk, and he was slipping into a coma. Wayne was praying with us.

That was the most emotional moment I've experienced in my life, and thank God that Wayne was there to stand me up because I couldn't do it alone. I just remember Wayne was praying for his soul and saying, "Let's go, Roger!"

It was so powerful to experience that with Wayne and the Life Flight pilots. The doctor said, "Roger can hear you, tell *him* this stuff." Every time I would mention the kids' names, "Race and Siena, we love you, you fight," Roger's body would react, and I knew he could hear me.

Within hours, the swelling was taking over his brain. Wayne went home and got LaVerne and the whole crew–Kenny, my bosses Sonya Thompson and Tony Garbo, and producer Jenn Charlton and my crew all came to the hospital, and we all waited together.

Surgeons removed part of the left side of Roger's skull because his brain was swelling at an alarming rate. Had they not done that, he would've died that night. We all prayed together, but Wayne led those prayers all night.

I knew he truly cared for me when he dropped everything on a Friday night to be there for me, my children, and Roger—especially since he had been awake since maybe 2AM the previous morning.

In the last ten years, I've experienced disappointments, sadness, and heart-break. There were times I would be crying in the green room, and Wayne would hug me and say, "C'mon let's go, get in that studio. People need you, so put on a happy face."

He's just as proud and supportive of my kids as I am. My kids adore Wayne and LaVerne, and Danielle is like a sister to Siena. We are family, and as I said before, Wayne and I would take a bullet for each other.

It feels weird saying he's just a friend because he is the best friend that anyone can have. When I say he's a brother, I mean that in my heart.

Wayne and I have covered a lot of big stories together. The biggest story going into September 11, 2001, was that Michael Jordan was coming out of retirement. That is until we saw the first plane crash. Then, we saw the second plane as we were on TV talking with our viewers, trying to make sense of what we were seeing. Our coverage of the aftermath of the 9/11 attacks continued for weeks.

We've covered school shootings and other terrible incidents. We could look at each other, and without saying a word, we knew what each other was thinking. We've relied on each other to get through some tough stories.

But I've also had some of my most fun moments with Wayne. He's so funny and fun-loving, and we're always laughing together.

He's also touched so many lives, and his giving spirit is amazing! Anyone who knows Wayne will tell you he's a sweet, humble guy with a huge heart. He always talks about the incredible values that his mom Annie instilled in him, and his brother Will.

Wayne could easily have that superstar mentality, but what he does with his church is Christ-like. And on most weekends, he's raising money or giving away coats and turkey dinners. He still makes time for that, and he could be at his house in Florida every weekend if he wanted to be there. I love that he talks the talk and walks the walk. He wants to make a difference, so he walks among everyone and the people that need him the most. He will never turn his back on people.

That says so much about Wayne and the love and support he has for his family. LaVerne's just amazing, and she is his rock. I know that she and their children, his daughters, and Will's family have all come together to support that. It's centered around Wayne because it is his mission, and it's just amazing.

I'm so proud of him.

# Chapter 19

# Richard "Zoom" Scott
## Camera Operator in SkyFox, Wayne's Friend for 40 years

I transferred from the University of Toledo to Kent State University in the spring of 1979 as a communications major. Everyone in the communications department was talking about this guy named Wayne Dawson. Even the ladies kept bringing him up, and I was like, "Hold on now! I got to meet this Wayne Dawson," but he wasn't there anymore.

I figured I would just take over Wayne's ladies since he was gone. Somebody needed to fill in during his absence, and I was able and willing. Since I was in the broadcasting industry as he had been, I met a friend of his named Darryl Hill, and he told me that Wayne was doing a video for him and asked me if I wanted to meet him. I said, "Heck yeah, I want to meet Wayne Dawson!" So, we rode to East Cleveland, where Wayne was living at the time, and I walked in and introduced myself. It was obvious that Wayne was a big deal.

We stayed in touch with each other even though I went to Channel 5 shortly thereafter. A couple of years later, the opportunity arose for me to work at Channel 8, and the only person I knew there was Wayne.

We've had a great relationship over the years and bonded right off the bat. I didn't realize that it would last this long because there was plenty of iconic talent at that station. From Big Chuck and Little John to the late great Dick Goddard, Wayne fit right in, and he's literally one of the best friends that a man could ever have. He's friends with a lot of people, but when Wayne calls someone his friend, it really means something.

At first, Wayne was working afternoons, and I worked the morning show. Then, we were both on weekends, and we would see each other and talk. He was transferred to the morning show after about five or ten years, but we remained friends.

Wayne was the host of a community affairs show called *Neighborhood,* and it was one of the best shows of its kind in the country. Wayne, myself, and Herb Thomas (who was Wayne's boy) became like the Three Musketeers. I felt that we were unstoppable with that show, and we won Emmys together–that's how good the show was.

Wayne was a heck of a writer, and he still is, which is something he learned at Kent State. He cut his teeth the way that you're supposed to, from the ground up. Right after leaving Kent State, he was put into a program specifically for blacks to work in the industry at an early age by our general manager at the time, Virgil Dominic. That catapulted Wayne to who he is today.

One of his main talents was that he could write and tell a story and take pictures to make it all work together. I remember praying together before he went on the air every morning, and then he would be brilliant.

I've learned a lot about Wayne along the way, such as his love for East Cleveland, where he grew up. He's a heck of a dresser and a handsome guy, which is why the ladies loved him.

I'm so grateful that he and I clicked right away and we're both still in it grinding 37 years later. It's been a friendship that's beyond words because it's grounded in spirituality and love for one another, black man to black man, brother to brother.

When Wayne lost his father, I was at the funeral, and he thanked me for coming. It was the same thing when he lost his mom. I knew the family background and his brother, Will Dawson, whom I love tremendously as well.

It was funny watching Wayne as a ladies' man before he was married. I'll never forget when he told me that he and LaVerne were getting married.

I was so excited that I called one of my friends in the radio business and told him that Wayne Dawson was getting married, and he should make a big announcement on the radio about that. Well, he did make that big announcement on the radio unbeknownst to Wayne—and you want to talk about a brother who was not happy with me! I figured all the ladies out there should know that Wayne was getting married.

I tell him to this day that I did that because I was just so happy for him, and he tells me that he does not remember that at all. I can laugh about it now, but he was so mad at me at the time and there's only been a few occasions in all these years that he has been mad, but mostly it has been nothing but love.

Wayne is a guy that leaves a positive impression on everybody because he is very charismatic, and he cares. He loves being a Shaw Cardinal and a Kent State Flasher more than anything, and it's all about winning with Wayne. He loves his Cavs and his Browns. He's all about anything with Cleveland. A couple of years ago, he took part in the King for a Day celebration during homecoming that kicked off the party at Kent State. They've honored him many times at KSU, and I've gone there many times to see him win awards. He's really proud that he graduated from Shaw High School and Kent State University.

On Memorial Day, Wayne was always Grand Marshall of the parade with the Shaw Cardinals, and people love him everywhere he goes. He doesn't always know people that come up to him, but everybody knows him, and that's the beauty of it. People would always tell him that they watch him every morning.

Back in the day when LeBron James was playing here, we'd go to the games. Wayne would always get the VIP treatment, and everybody was excited, yelling, "Hey Wayne Dawson is here!" The officials would take his coat and hang it in the back room. He never gets a big head about any of that, and he stays pretty level. I remind him that he's *the* Wayne Dawson, and I'm rolling with him!

It makes me feel good to hear kids, older people, and younger people say, "Man, I watch you every morning." Wayne attracts that attention from everybody. He's one of a kind, and I am happy to say that he's ours. All of Cleveland says that; it's not just me. I've held fashion shows, something called "Soup for the Soul," and other non-profit organizations that I started, and Wayne would be in awe of me because I was giving back to the community.

That prompted him to use his own power and influence to give more visibility to the Dawson Foundation. I said, "Wayne, you've got a half-million people watching you on the morning show every day. You can do anything you want!" They give away coats, hats, and boots for kids. Soon, companies started throwing money at the foundation to help.

It speaks volumes about Wayne that no matter who he sits next to in the air chair, the ratings would be the same. He's still the consummate professional no matter who his co-anchor is. He gets to the set early and reads over his script about ten to fifteen minutes before the show. He's still that professional I met almost 40 years ago who could talk to anyone and come up with a story because his interviewing skills are second to none.

He's easily in the same class as Lester Holt.

The spiritual side of Wayne is an entirely different dynamic of him that many people never saw coming. It goes back to when he and I would pray every morning before the show. When God calls, you must listen, and Wayne listened. Not many people can juggle their life being an on-air talent of a major network in the 18$^{th}$ market in the country while being the pastor of a church. The dynamic of that is unbelievable, but Wayne does it out of love.

He says, "The church could never pay me what I'm making at Fox 8," and he's right. But his spirituality and his "payment" is done with serving the Lord, and he is a servant. If anything happened at the station back in the day, people would go to Wayne Dawson to pray.

Virgil Dominic put Wayne and the rest of us on the path to success. He noticed Wayne's talent at a young age, and he knew it would last a lifetime. This hand-picked minority young man is still working hard every day, waking up at 2 AM and going to the gym after the morning show. Who does that?

When Wayne told me that he was going to become the pastor at Grace, I attended his ordination, and it was remarkable. Pastors from all over flocked to participate in him becoming a minister of the gospel, and I sat back and marveled at him doing his first sermon. He knows how to make things work for the betterment of people. To matriculate from where he was to where he is now is phenomenal.

Wayne is also a teacher, and I've learned a lot from him, including many of my interviewing skills and how to talk to people. He has a knack for asking the right questions and getting people to talk. Virgil nabbed him early, but Wayne could have easily been a network star on NBC, ABC, or CBS because he's that good, and I've told him that for many years.

His response: "Cleveland."

He loves Cleveland and will always be one of Cleveland's Own. He's been saying, "Welcome to the dawn of a new day" for years on the morning show, but the news director picked up on it only about a year ago and said, "We've got to use that!" So, when I'm in the helicopter, I film the sun coming up, predicated on what Wayne has been saying for a long time.

When history judges Wayne and what he meant to this world, he will be remembered as a man of service to our God. He picked up his cross and followed, and he led by example. He is led by the things that are unseen, and he is led by our Lord and Savior Jesus Christ to the utmost because that's who he is. Little did we know that he was going to be that, and it's been a remarkable ride. He's been led by the spirit.

Wayne's story is one-of-a-kind, and there's never been a person in our lifetime like him. Wayne bleeds his community, and as I've said before: he loves Shaw and Kent State.

There is nobody bigger at our station than Wayne Dawson. When I'm out in the field covering various stories, people ask for two people: Wayne Dawson and Kenny Crumpton! When Dick Goddard left this earth, God had already put Wayne in position at the station.

Goddard used to do the Christmas thing with the Cleveland Orchestra, but I looked up last year, and I saw Wayne doing it. There's nobody bigger in this city than him, period. His relationship with LeBron and his mom, Gloria James... they knew Wayne from when he interviewed LeBron years ago. Both he and his mom grew up in Akron watching Wayne and Gloria used to say, "I love Wayne Dawson."

# Chapter 20

# April Sutton
Former Classmate at KSU and Co-Worker at *Newscenter 8*

I met Wayne Dawson at Kent State University during my second year there. Like me, he majored in telecommunications. My first memory of Wayne is seeing him walking around campus carrying a portable blue typewriter.

"Who is this guy walking around with this blue typewriter?" I thought to myself. He looked like he was prepared to do a news report on the spot. I soon learned he was in telecommunications and was interested in being a journalist. Wayne was also the anchorman for the TV2 news studio (as it was called) at Kent State University.

I was doing a talk show on campus for TV2 called "Reflections" while Wayne did the news. One thing was clear to everybody: Wayne was a natural and already looked like a seasoned anchorman. He had the mannerisms down, and the voice, tone, and ability to write the news appeared to come so easily. He was undeniably the most talented of all of us aspiring to have a career in television.

I knew unequivocally that Wayne would get hired, get a job in television, and be a successful anchorman. He would write news stories while doing a radio show and always took the time to make sure that he was diving into every element of broadcasting and journalism.

Wayne and I both graduated from Kent State in 1979 and subsequently had the good fortune of being in the right places at the right times to help get our careers started. At the time, I worked part-time at the Board of

Education in Akron, and the co-superintendent was Virgil Dominic's brother.

Virgil Dominic was an incredibly important figure in broadcast television and the news director at *Newscenter 8*. I was lucky enough to get a recommendation from a woman named Ann Gates, and she let Virgil's brother know that I was getting my degree in television.

When I found out that Mr. Dominic in Akron was related to Mr. Dominic at Channel 8, I asked Mrs. Gates to introduce me to Virgil's brother so that I might be able to get a one-on-one interview with Virgil.

Mr. Dominic called his brother and said, "There's a girl here named April who would like to get an interview with you because she's getting her degree in television."

Virgil agreed, and I got the interview at Channel 8.

At the time, the station was looking for two African-Americans for "The Minority Training Program," which existed to get more minorities into the broadcast television field. Ironically, during my interview with Virgil, he asked if I knew anyone at my university that I thought might be a good choice to join me in the program as an intern at Channel 8.

"Absolutely!" I said without any hesitation.

"He would be the best intern or young and up-and-coming hire. His name is Wayne Dawson."

Seeing my enthusiasm, Virgil asked if I could get him to come to the TV station.

"You have to get yourself together. Get a suit, white shirt, and a tie because you have an interview with Virgil Dominic at Channel 8," I said to Wayne, unable to hide my enthusiasm.

Wayne was like, "What?!" And that's how he ended up at Channel 8, and I'm happy and proud to say that he's been there ever since. He's had an unbelievably successful career in television which is very uncommon because the TV industry is a revolving door. Often, people sign a two-year contract, and when it ends, they are released and must try to find another TV job in another television market. Wayne has stayed in Cleveland, Ohio since 1979, and that's a remarkable testament to his talent.

Wayne and I were hired as part-time employees on the same day. It was a wonderful experience because it allowed us to go right into a major television market. Channel 8 was a very popular TV station and still is today, so it was a perfect training ground for Wayne and for me. I left Channel 8 after about two years, but I have always kept in touch with Wayne because he's like family to me.

Over the years, my family would watch him on TV and tell me what a great job he was doing. It was exciting to know that he was still at Channel 8 and having a great career. My mother adopted (in her mind) Wayne as her godson, and she would tell everybody, "Wayne Dawson is my godson." She was very proud of him and watched him on television regularly.

I marvel at Wayne's 43 years at one station because it is so rare. Since he is so extremely talented, thorough, and a very serious journalist, his longevity doesn't surprise me. He takes his career very seriously, and he's always understood his lane. He's good at being in the spotlight while remaining in the shadows simultaneously. That's a very different dynamic, and I think that anyone in a high-profile position should be able to do that because it allows others to shine.

Wayne's humility goes back to our days at TV2 when he was doing the news at Kent State University. You never got the feeling that he thought that he was more talented or better than the other students, and everyone liked and admired him. Much of that was because of his humble spirit, which he's carried deep into adulthood. He is a down-to-earth, super nice man who won't have many enemies because of the way he is.

One of the biggest thrills for me is what I experienced while in his presence. Seeing people stop him and want to take a picture with him or ask him for an autograph just knocked me out. It's been exciting to watch his evolution from Kent State to Channel 8.

Whether he's putting gas in his car, going to a restaurant, or to church, he is a highly recognizable individual and is a bona fide Cleveland, Ohio celebrity. People get excited to see Wayne Dawson in person, and it always makes me proud to see how far he's come in his life and his career. It's wonderful to see him be so gracious to the many people who acknowledge him.

I used to call Wayne "the Walter Cronkite of TV2" at Kent State University, so it was destiny for him to become a real broadcast journalist on television.

Wayne Dawson's enduring legacy will be that he is one of the greatest television broadcasters that ever entered the industry in Cleveland, Ohio. He maintained his position as a solid anchorman and morning host and is a very spiritual man who understands that his career came as a blessing from God.

He has never forgotten that, and it is very clear that his career didn't just come to him—it came from the hand of God and from the womb when Wayne was born. He was destined to be a television broadcaster.

# Chapter 21

# Dr. R.A. Vernon
## Founder and Senior Pastor of the Word Church

Wayne Dawson is the G.O.A.T. (greatest of all time) of morning talk show hosts in Cleveland, so it is almost impossible not to be acquainted with him, at least subconsciously, if you live in Cleveland because he's the face you wake up to each morning. He's a few years older than me, so I've been waking up to his face on the news since my teenage years, whether I was at Mom's house, Dad's house, or Grandma's house.

He's like a family member, similar to how many people see Kobe Bryant. People wonder why there was such an emotional impact when Kobe passed away tragically and suddenly. It was like you knew him and grew up with him, so people were in awe as to why his death had such an emotional impact on them when they had never met him. It's easy to feel as though you're forming a bond with someone you watch daily.

As our church began to have an impact in the city, we were constantly being interviewed by Fox 8 for some giveaways we were doing to impact the city. Wayne frequently interviewed me, and through that, we began to bond.

One of the hidden secrets that some don't know about Wayne is that he is so much more than an on-air personality. Of course, that's his occupation and how he feeds his children, but in terms of his *vocation*, he is a pastor, minister, and philanthropist, and he hosts a bowling event each year that I've been privileged enough to attend a couple of times.

Graduating from the great Shaw High School in East Cleveland, Ohio, he is familiar with those on the margins. As Jesus said plain and simple, "I was hungry, you fed me. I was in prison, you came to see me." We call it Matthew 25, Alive at the Word Church. He said that in Matthew 25, "We believe," how do we bring that alive? It's one thing for it to be in a holy writ, but how do you bring scripture alive in terms of philanthropy and give Jesus legs?

To me, that's what Wayne has always done, from coat giveaways with his brother through their foundation. I know him not only as a news personality but as a man of God. I believe passion cannot be manipulated or faked. God gives certain persons a passion for philanthropy—the scripture talks about a gift of giving—that I think God has blessed me or led me towards. The gifts are available to all Christians, but I think there tends to be one gift that God flashes through you more than others. You've probably heard that *your misery becomes your ministry.*

Growing up in the projects of Cleveland, I don't think Wayne dealt with as much poverty as I did. But to me, when you're from the projects and your mother was young when she had you, it makes you *want* to give back. Wayne has always exemplified this need, saying, "I made it big here in Cleveland; I'm not going to forget the place I come from."

I was a bit surprised when Wayne became a pastor only because I am a fellow clergyman, and I know the laborious, arduous, difficult task of pastoring, particularly in a traditional context. Because Wayne was so successful at what he was doing, and he's handsome and young-looking, I had to bring a perspective that others could not.

I asked him, "Do you really want this, for lack of a better word, headache?" Transforming a traditional church requires patience and time. There are two kinds of pastors: founding pastors and transitional pastors.

Founding pastors like myself will walk into a high school with nothing but a keyboard and a microphone and start preaching and singing and enticing people to start coming. A transitional pastor goes to an established church that's set in its ways.

I was concerned about him enjoying the evening time of his life because he's earned that, but him being who he is, he felt led to take on this challenge, and from what I can see, he's done okay.

I met Wayne after he had been changed. The only Wayne I know is the God-fearing, on fire for God, gentleman, philanthropist, and a smooth criminal on that television. Speaking from a Christian perspective, when God gets ahold of a man's life, some things just come with wisdom.

At a certain level, you fall and do dumb stuff that impacts you and those closest to you. If R.A. Vernon or Wayne Dawson has a public scandal, it will impact thousands in Cleveland. So, we have a large responsibility not only to honor God but us and our families because so many could fall or be impacted negatively if we did something out of character.

He and I, in that sense, are somewhat analogous and are maybe two of the most recognized black faces in Cleveland, Ohio. Me because of the size of our ministry and having been on television the past 20 years, and him being on television the past 40 years.

Mayors come and go. LeBron came and went. But in terms of staying power and stick-to-it-iveness, arguably, he and I are probably the most known black faces in our city. With that comes a responsibility, and maybe that's why we relate to each other so well.

Native Clevelanders such as Steve Harvey and Arsenio Hall may be more popular nationally and internationally, but their impact in Cleveland has not been felt like we've felt the impact of Wayne Dawson.

Wayne was born here and has given his whole life to this city, and that puts him at number one in that category.

When a person has been on television as much as Wayne Dawson, a smooth black brother who's probably the best dressed man in Cleveland, he's going to stand out.

His enduring legacy will be that he's powerful yet humble, which is a rare combination. Wayne has a gentleness that makes you feel at ease in his presence that I envy as a pastor. Again, he's probably the most recognizable, black man in our city.

And yet, you cannot encounter him without sensing his humility and noticing how he makes everyone feel at ease. You never feel like you're in the presence of some mega news personality, but Wayne has an innate ability to make you feel like you're the only person in the room.

He has the fruit of the spirit. He most embodies gentleness and kindness; he exudes that, and you can tell it's natural. He doesn't have to fight to do it, and there's not a narcissistic bone in his body.

His legacy will be that he's a powerful man who loves the city of Cleveland and always carried himself like the ultimate gentleman.

# Chapter 22

# Crystal Webb
## Wayne's Second Oldest Daughter

My earliest memories of my dad start after my parents separated. I was in the third or fourth grade, and I didn't really understand what was happening until much later.

To their credit, when my parents were together, they never let me or my sister see them arguing. We always did holidays and birthdays together, and they did a good job of making things as normal as they could, even while they were having their issues as a couple.

Dad would pick me up at Mom's house on the weekends in a sports car. We would spend the entire Saturday together after he went to the gym or got a haircut earlier that morning. We'd listen to Phil Collins on the radio and my favorite song of his was, "Something Happened on the Way to Heaven." I loved that song so much that I picked it for us to dance to together at my wedding. Dad would always play gospel music, but Kirk Franklin was his favorite.

After lunch, Dad and I would visit my stepmom after work, then go to dinner. That was our Saturday together—just him and I.

I really liked LaVerne when I met her because she was very nice. She has always been the sweetest woman. She never made me or my sister feel like stepchildren, even after she and my dad had a daughter together. Some women in that situation would just say, "Whatever," about the other kids.

Around the same time my dad and LaVerne were getting married, I started to realize that he was a well-known public figure. During fifth or sixth grade, my friends were like, "I saw your dad on the news!" At first, it was cool, but after a while, it got annoying because some girls would say to me, "You think you're all that because your dad's on the news," and I was like, "Um, no." There was no reason for me to think it was a big deal because that's all he had done since I've been in this world. He didn't raise my sister and me to be arrogant, and his mindset was that our behavior was a reflection on him.

His image was important to his career, so we didn't want to ever do anything that would embarrass him. Some of my classmates were jealous, and others admired him and would ask for his autograph. People would ask me, "How does it feel to have your dad on the news?" and I would say, "How does it feel to have your dad work at a bank?" It just was what it was.

Dad is the same person in front of the cameras or away from them. What you see is what you get, whether he's on the news or sitting in his house. He's always there to listen, and he always has a good story. He may be a little more of a jokester when it's just us, but he's always just been the supportive loving guy that you see on the news.

But if he was disappointed in us, oh you'd know! I hated when he said he was disappointed in me because I never wanted to disappoint my dad. No matter what we did, he would always show his love for us.

It hit differently when Dad was upset with me than it did when Mom was.

When I started dating, my dad was not overbearing but he did have rules. When I had a boyfriend in high school, he would never say his name, he would refer to him as my "friend." He'd say, "Your friend has to be gone by ten." Also, if my dad wasn't awake when I got home from a date, I always wanted to make sure that he knew I was home. Even though he never yelled or cussed at me, he had a way of letting me know he was mad without saying it, and I never wanted to see that side of him.

He was always open to meeting my "friends," but he had a slick and cool way of handling things like that. When I got married to my first husband, my dad didn't necessarily approve of him. I had gotten pregnant, which is why we decided to get married.

"Chris, you can just have the baby," my dad said to me at the time. He wasn't disappointed that I got pregnant and never talked down to me about that, but he tried to convince me not to get married. I felt that he didn't want me to be happy, but he felt that we were too young and immature.

To his credit, he still walked me down the aisle.

My husband and I were young and broke with a baby, but Dad helped when he could. When my first husband and I divorced, my dad was very supportive and always asked what I needed. He allowed me and his two grandsons to live with him, always making his position clear without talking down to me.

Dad loves my current husband, mostly because he's really active in church, studies the Bible, and has a relationship with God. He saw that my husband was not coddled as a child and he liked that my husband went to him first and said, "I want to marry your daughter."

It's no surprise that my father, who is a pastor, would like my church-going husband. People ask me if I was ever surprised that he went into the ministry, but I knew that it was coming because Dad spoke at a different church every Sunday when I was younger, so we never committed to one.

He attended Bethany Baptist Church for a while, and I knew he was working to find a church that he could pastor full-time. Each Sunday was like a tour, and I've always thought that Dad's speaking skills were amazing. Sometimes, his sermons were the same as the previous week, so I found ways to keep my attention on him, such as timing the length of his speech.

I would also count the number of times that he used the word "um," which was usually only once during his presentation. He was so good, natural, and trained that it was as if he was just having a conversation. When I lived with him for a while, I watched him type his sermons word-for-word in size 48 font and roll through his speech while barely looking at the paper.

I was fascinated that he found new things to talk about each week, but it's not surprising because Dad studies. He's always reading a book and he still records his morning shows and watches them when he gets home from work to critique his "performance."

My dad's work ethic is so strong that I'm influenced by it in my career at University Hospital. He's evolved in his 43 years at Channel 8 to where they don't want to let him go. There was a point when everyone was crazy about his suits and would tune in to see what Wayne Dawson was wearing. He's always been open to changing with the times and trying new things while keeping his swag. When they took away his show *Neighborhood*, he went from nights to mornings, and he just rolled with it and never showed his frustration. His verbal delivery continues to get better, and he's been more comfortable with himself.

Fox 8 won't be the same when he finally decides to retire because there's something about Wayne Dawson that makes people want to see him and they look forward to it every morning. Sometimes he acts silly and dances. People want to see that in the morning.

Dad is a people person, and he loves when people share their stories with him. He's always trying to give back, especially to Cleveland because the city has given him so much. A lot of people want to get out of Cleveland, but Dad has made such an impact on the place where he was born. It's obvious that he wants to make the best out of the city and do his part.

When young kids and older black men see him on the streets in his jeans talking, just the fact that anyone can walk up and talk to him could change somebody's life. A lot of times, we see people on TV who are arrogant–Dad has every right to be that way, and he's not. Just being who he is shows the love he has for the city where he's lived his whole life.

The impression my dad has left on his grandkids will be his legacy. He loves his grandkids, and he wants them to be the black excellence that they can be. That doesn't mean they have to be newscasters, but whatever they decide to do, Dad wants them to do it to the best of their ability.

He stresses working hard, putting themselves out there, and being confident in whatever they decide to do. He's set such a high standard for all of us, but because of the love and encouragement, it makes us want to reach his standard and go beyond it. He wants them to go for whatever they want, but to always put God first.

# Chapter 23

# Deante Young
## Author/co-writer of this book

In June 2021, I had the bold and crazy idea to ask Wayne Dawson to let me interview him for what became my third book in six months. The problem was, I didn't know Wayne and the likelihood that he would agree to this request felt more impossible than doing jumping jacks while wearing handcuffs!

But since the book I wanted him to appear in was titled *Winning is For Losers!* I decided to take my own advice and try to "win" his participation while putting myself in a position to possibly "lose" if he turned me down. We had a mutual friend, so I asked her to introduce us.

Three months later, my book was released, and it contained a chapter from the man himself. Wayne said "Yes," and my life was forever changed for the better because of that serendipitous moment when I chose to ignore the fear of failure and reach out to him.

I look back on that day with a profound sense of—embarrassment. I use that word because I now understand how ridiculous it was for me to be afraid to ask Wayne to help with something. He *always* wants to help people! Since we connected, I have grown exceedingly fond of this great man because he is so much better than his highlights.

Wayne Dawson, a man who has epitomized journalistic exceptionalism for 43 years and counting, is my friend. Sure, his trophy case illustrates his long-standing proficiency as not only a reporter and anchorman; but also, as a steadfast activist and community leader who handles his personal and professional life like an elite NBA point guard.

He almost always makes the right play and quickly corrects his mistakes.

Like the rest of Northeast Ohio, I have watched Wayne on television for many moons, going as far back as the days of the Reagan White House in the era of Rubik's Cubes and Ms. Pac-Man. In that respect, Wayne is forever immortalized as a member of all our families.

I admire this extraordinary man for many reasons. He possessed such certainty as a child that he would someday become something massive in this world, possibly the president of the United States. He never viewed his ethnicity as a deterrent to any of his aspirations because he believed that he could achieve greatness on his own merits.

That self-belief was very uncommon for a black person, especially during the turbulent 1960s when he grew up in a world dragged down by the bitter reality of institutional racism. I also admire the special relationship that young Wayne had with his mother and grandparents because they infused him with the mindset that would eventually guide him to carrying out his purpose.

The surreal circumstances of his life during the six-year period from 1968 to 1974 only prepared him for the trials and tribulations that he was destined to endure as he climbed the mountain of success.

His household, once a haven of endless inspiration and good intentions, became a broken home supported by government benefits and rife with heartbreak. Possibly as a refuge, teenage Wayne traded his excellent academic performances for a life of hanging with drug addicts and womanizers.

And he became one of them.

But the powerful influence that his mother and grandparents held over him as a child was always embedded in his soul. Wayne straightened up his act and moved toward his goals with the uncompromising force of a tractor-trailer barreling down a highway.

He excelled and honed his craft for years in college before becoming a breakout star with Cleveland's *Newscenter 8* in 1980. The sheer unlikelihood that his trajectory from age 13 to 25 would culminate in uncommon and immediate success deserves a standing ovation.

But despite all of Wayne's illustrious accomplishments, his enduring celebrity in Northeast Ohio, and his ultra-stylish fashion sense, the man himself is a winning human being from the inside out.

On the evening of Saturday, May 14, 2022, Dawson and his lovely wife, Mrs. LaVerne, arrived at an elegant party center to fulfill a commitment that he'd made to me months earlier. The launch event for my 5th book, *Speak Before You Think!* took place that day, and Wayne was scheduled to interview me about my books in front of the people in attendance.

For almost an hour, the veteran journalist asked me various questions ranging in subject matter from how I got my start as a writer to my often-unusual personal style.

What made Wayne's appearance most impressive to me was the fact that he received a late invite to a ceremony at which he would receive an award that same night, and he opted to stay with me and sprinkle magic on *my* evening.

He even patiently posed for photographs after the interview and chatted with others as if he were nobody important. *That* polished skill is precisely what makes him somebody special because it illustrates his selflessness and humility.

As I've gotten to know Wayne, I am amazed that every great thing people say about him is true. He always makes a person feel like they are important to him; he is disarming, charismatic, and has a heart of gold. He always wants to help make someone's day a little better.

When I mentioned to Wayne that I had been receiving donations and sponsorships for my book launch event in February, he immediately volunteered to help and wrote me a check. It's refreshing and exciting to meet someone that's so highly accomplished, but still embodies humanity and kindness. It's rare in the television business, and it's rare in real life.

Wayne's sense of humor is incredible and highly underrated. I have laughed hard at many things he has said on the air and in our private conversations. Being in his presence is exciting, and there's a distinctive aura of charm and elegance that he gives off, yet he also projects an Everyman persona that attracts almost everyone.

His unyielding love for the essential people in his life—God first, then his children, grandchildren, wife, and the rest of humanity, is obvious and remarkable. He is the ultimate ally to those closest to him, and he handles that huge responsibility with a seriousness almost unprecedented in interpersonal relationships.

When Wayne said he considers me a friend, it felt like a gift from above. He also told me that I'm going to one day "be a big name," and God put him "in [my] path to help get [me] there." I was shocked at the power of his words, but more importantly, his belief in me.

Getting to know Cleveland's Own Wayne Dawson has been the blessing of a lifetime, and his transformative nature has already massively impacted my life and my thinking. I hope that I've been worthy of the time he has spent and invested in me.

What an awesome friend.

# Part IV: Reflection

In team sports, the final section of a game is typically the fourth quarter (or ninth inning in baseball). The best players often finish off the biggest games with a flourish; making key shots or passes in basketball, stealing a base or crushing a home run in baseball, throwing or rushing for a touchdown in football.

You get the idea.

Wayne Dawson has been a lifelong sports fan and he is certainly a big game player in his personal, spiritual and professional life. This final section of the book features quick, succinct chapters as Wayne dishes the dirty truth on what it takes to become a success in broadcasting and any other worthy endeavor.

He also reveals the origins of his world-class fashion sense, his plans for retirement and his love for his Fox 8 family. As a special treat, he includes a collection of personal photographs which depict key moments and individuals throughout his life's journey.

It's safe to say that Wayne Dawson closes this game—I mean, book, with a grand slam home run and an all-net 3-point shot from half court.

Please, hold your applause.

-D.Y.

# Chapter 24

# Survival of the Fittest

*"It is not the strongest of the species that survives,*
*nor the most intelligent.*
*It is the one that is most adaptable to change."*
—Charles Darwin

I'm often asked for advice on succeeding in the broadcasting industry, and there is no simple answer. Everybody is different, and we all take different paths to get into this business, but I will share what's worked for me over the years. I hope that it will inspire you to realize that you have the seeds of greatness within you, but you must be willing to make the necessary sacrifices to harvest those seeds.

You must show up every day and give 110% effort. That's the key; giving your best effort, which is always my goal. Every day, you must strive to get better and always try to improve. You will get hit with different things, racism or something else, but you can't let that stop you or use it as an excuse. You can't use being black as an excuse, or being from the eastside of Cleveland, living in an unstable or a single-parent household.

You've got to work beyond those circumstances and put your faith in God. You must ask God to lead you and guide you. Do what you can do and leave the rest to the Lord. That's been a key to my success. Always remember that you and God are a winning combination; that's how I look at life. The key is working hard, showing up every day, and autographing your work with greatness and your best abilities. Don't do anything halfway.

I always wanted to be the best writer, interviewer, and anchorman. Remember what I said about my elementary school years? Even then, I wanted to be the best, and I looked around at the other kids to see who my competition was until I started falling off track. That competitive spirit was there initially, and you must have a competitive spirit in broadcasting because it's a competitive business and everybody wants your job.

Everyone wants to be an anchorperson and sit at the desk. You must always be on your game because so much is out of your control. If your ratings are not good, or you tick somebody off, you'll get taken off the desk. If you have good ratings but you are a bad employee, they can take you off.

We've been number one for all 23 years that I've been on the morning show, and that's a beautiful thing. When I took over, they were already number one, and despite some people thinking the ratings were going to fall, they didn't. We were blessed, and to God be the glory.

You must constantly remind yourself that you'll have to "crawl before you can walk." You might feel that some individuals were promoted quicker than you, but the race doesn't go to the swift, it goes to the person that stays the course, and that's been my story. Others came after me and were promoted ahead of me, but I kept doing my thing, and 43 years later, I'm still there doing it.

Most of the individuals I started with are not even in the business anymore because it's fleeting. I'm only there because I'm dogmatic and determined to succeed like my life depends on it in whatever I do. Nobody has given me anything, but any break I've ever gotten, I've taken advantage of it. If somebody opens the door for you, run through it.

It's like my guy, the great Chicago Bears running back Gale Sayers used to say, "Give me eighteen inches of daylight. That's all I need." He would drive his point home by adding, "Just give me a crack, and I'm darting through that bad boy." That's how I've looked at my life and my television career; give me an opportunity and with God's help, I'll take it from there.

As I've said many times, my mom gave me great confidence and self-belief early on and practicing in the mirror was just an outcome of wanting to be the best. I was reading in the mirror and recording myself while being critical of my performance, all because I wanted to be the best.

That was all part of the process of becoming an acceptable broadcaster. It goes back to my first few years at Channel 8 when Tony Ballew told me I had a "black dialect." I could've taken his opinion and had a bad attitude about it, but I was like, "Really? Okay." They sent me to speech school, and I just rolled with it. It is what it is and you must take your opportunities and run with them.

I talked about my high school job at the Forum Cafeteria when I wanted to be the best dishwasher there. When I worked at Eastern Star Home, I thought about what Dr. King said about being a street sweeper and doing it like Michelangelo. Whatever you do, strive to be the best at it. It takes dedication.

Some people in television have things given to them, but I've always had to work for mine. They're not going to give a black man from the east side of Cleveland anything, and I'm glad I had to work to get here. I'm not a beautiful woman, I'm just a brother from the hood, so I've got to go get mine. I'm not even that good-looking of a guy like Clark Gable, Billy Dee Williams, or Denzel Washington. I just do what I do.

Speaking of Denzel, I have so much respect for him because he talks a lot about putting God first. That's the key to this whole thing.

# Chapter 25

# Clean

*"Elegance is when the inside is as beautiful as the outside."*
—Coco Chanel

My clothing style has long been a source of curiosity for some folks and even, can I say–flattery to me? But it is what it is, and I don't mind sharing the genesis of what I've heard people call my "fashion sense." I don't think the story is that interesting, but nevertheless, here it goes.

At one time, I was not a good dresser. I was the king of sports jackets, and I thought I was clean. In the black community, we often refer to being or looking "clean" as nice or sharp in appearance or attire. So, while I thought I was clean, my daughter Tammy had other ideas.

She was living with me at the time, and ever since I got into the business, I would study my tapes and critique them (newscasts) after they aired. One day, I was at home watching a tape of one of my newscasts. Tammy happened to be in the room, and she looked at my image on the TV screen and said, "Dad!" and giggled. She then asked, "Dad, what are you wearing? You need to spruce up your wardrobe!" This was sometime in the mid-90s, I'd say '95 or '96 when she was about 20.

I looked at Tammy like, "I don't know what you're talking about. I'm clean," I said proudly. When she told me I needed to upgrade my wardrobe, it went in one ear and out the other because I wasn't trying to hear that. Our news director at the time was a woman named Kathy Williams, and she brought in consultants to look at the tapes of me and my co-workers to critique our on-air performance.

They also brought in consultants to critique our clothing. The woman who critiqued mine told me what color combinations she felt were best for me, and something clicked in my mind during that experience. I decided that I would step up my game in how I dressed. I began thinking about different color combinations and studying fashion magazines like GQ and any other fashion magazine I could find.

My plan then was to follow the latest trends, and that's how it all started. My daughter planted the seed, even though I initially rejected her opinion. But when the station brought in the professionals, it sparked my thinking, and I just dove into focusing on studying fashion and what individuals were wearing.

I'm also not afraid to take risks with my clothing choices, which sets me apart from others. Back in the day, I was the guy that wore colored shirts when they weren't very popular. I wore the four-button jackets when a lot of people weren't doing that because I had no problem taking risks–even now. But I've backed off from that a little bit nowadays, though I still do it on occasion.

Gradually, people began complimenting me for my clothing, so the idea that it was always there isn't true. My fashion reputation developed over time, and when I was a student at Shaw High School in the 70s, I wasn't an exquisite dresser, although my daughter says I "always dressed nice." Maybe I did, but I wasn't known for that until the past 20 years or so.

Growing up on the city's east side, I always had a *sense* of fashion, even when I was a kid. I remember when silk socks and Sansabelt pants were in. I used to hang around guys that could dress, especially this one guy named Preston Darling. He was always clean. I was in fifth or sixth grade, but I tried to model myself after him. Thinking about all that, I guess I always had some level of fashion sense, but it wasn't that noticeable until I modified my style after that moment at Channel 8.

When that happened, I decided that I would make a statement whenever I rolled up in the studio. I thought, "I'm going to push the envelope a little bit with my fashion," and I did. Of course, I was an anchorman by 1995, and under the bright lights of the studio, so my clothes were more visible. When I was a reporter, the way I dressed wasn't a big deal because I was out in the field doing my thing.

Being an anchor, that's when people notice more, even though they only see you from the waist up. Sometimes I would do the weekend show, and I'd be suited up from the waist up and have on a pair of shorts. There's a picture of us; me, Sissy, anchors Mark Koontz and Mark Schraeder and we're all clean from the waist up, but wearing shorts outside of camera view.

I was never into shoes until recently. I would always wear a suit and gym shoes because people can't see the shoes when I'm on the air. As I began making more public appearances and doing more preaching, I became more cognizant of my choices in shoes. A question I get asked often:

"How many suits do you have?"

I'd say, "At least 75."

# Chapter 26

# 50 Years in Television?

*"You have to prove that you know what you're doing. You have to have longevity. You have to stay around."*
—Venus Williams

When you spend 43 years at any job, questions start coming up about retirement. I'm still enjoying myself at Fox 8, but the thought about how much longer I will do this does cross my mind. Some people have asked me if I'll try to make it to 50, which is crazy to even think about! 50 years in television? That would make me 74 years old, not too far off from the legendary Dick Goddard. He was 85 when he retired in 2016 after 50 years on Cleveland television.

Broadcaster Leon Bibb, one of my role models, reached the 50-year milestone recently as well and he was in *his* seventies!

Whenever I retire, I'd like to do the "snowbird" thing: spend my winters in Florida and my summers in Cleveland. That's my prayer, and we'll see how things work out. After a certain age, everything depends on your health. If the Lord blesses me with health, that's what I plan to do.

I love Florida because it's easy to get to. After visiting there so often, I knew I wouldn't mind having a place in the Sunshine State, so I started looking at condos. My real estate agent told me that for what I'd pay for a condo, I might as well get a house, so I got a house.

I also have three timeshares; two in Florida and one in Williamsburg, Virginia, and I haven't used them since the pandemic. I still have the timeshare because they're like roaches. Once you get them, you can't get rid of them!

Career-wise, I could probably do five or six more years. Again, it depends on my health, but the idea of going another seven years on the air to get to 50 years–that's crazy. I wouldn't want to do the morning show that long where I'd still have to get up at 2 AM. I would love to do something like my old show, *Neighborhood*, but we'll see. It's always in God's hands on God's time.

# Chapter 27

# Morning Show Love

When I first started at Channel 8 in 1979, I was fresh out of college and eager to show what I could do. The station was controlled by one of three major national networks at the time; NBC was the national network version of Cleveland's local WKYC, ABC was the national network version of the local WEWS, and CBS was the network version of WJKW (later WJW) which is where I worked at Channel 8. The name of the newscasts was *Newscenter 8* which had been in effect for just two or three years when I joined the station.

WJW became a Fox affiliate in September 1994 and for us, the changes were noticeable. By October 1995, the newscasts were no longer branded as *Newscenter 8*. After several name changes ("Eight is News," for example) the newscasts were re-branded as "Fox 8 News" which of course, is what it remains today.

Prior to the switch in '94, Channel 8 in Cleveland, Ohio had been tied to a major network, which was CBS. Once that was no longer the case, it made all the difference in the world and even today, almost 30 years later, Fox has little primetime programming. The switch opened the door for us because we were able to do a lot more news and that holds true even now which is how we're able to do six hours of news on weekday mornings. We are not bound by what the network does like we were during the CBS years.

While other stations have to switch to their national morning shows, we are still on the air. In the evenings, it allows us to have the 10 o'clock news because other stations have primetime programming from 7 to 11PM.

Primetime on Fox is only two hours from 8 to 10PM, so we have a lot more flexibility. Back then when the change was made, we all thought it was going to be a negative, but it turned into a positive. Fox does a lot on cable television, but they don't do much network stuff and as I said, they only have two hours per night of primetime.

Of course, they have sports sometimes, but generally they have a smaller primetime schedule.

As I mentioned earlier, I started co-anchoring the morning show in 1999, and I'm still waking up at 2AM on weekdays to do it. The current group that I work with on *Fox 8 News in the Morning* are like family to me. The station, my co-anchors, management and many others behind the scenes help make my job much easier. I mostly anchor with Sissy and Kristi on weekday mornings, along with Todd Meany and good friend Kenny Crumpton, and our meteorologists Scott Sabol, Jenn Harcher, and Alexis Walters. We have a wonderful bond, like family, something the other stations have unsuccessfully tried to duplicate. The truth is simple: what we have is natural, nothing staged, nothing planned, it's just an outgrowth of the love and respect we have for each other. It's my belief that this natural camaraderie is why we've remained Cleveland's most watched newscast over the years.

Occasionally, I work with Jessica Dill, Stacey Frey and Natalie Herbick–all beautiful people inside and out. Kenny and of course Richard "Zoom" Scott are my brothers from another mother, and they know it. Patty Harken handles SkyFox like nobody's business and she's wonderful, funny, and a true joy to work with.

I also want to thank all the lovely women that I co-anchored with over many years: Rebecca Shaw, Robin Meade, Kelly O'Donnell, Laurie Jennings, Stefani Schaefer (three different stints!), Donna Douglas, Lorrie Taylor, Jacque Smith (now Jovic), Kathy Kronenberger, Tracy McCool and Kristi Capel. They all made life easier for me on the air and that's a beautiful thing.

When the station held a tribute to me in July 2022 to celebrate my 40 years as a full-time employee, I got choked up. I don't do any of this for the recognition, accolades or notoriety, but it was a blessing to be celebrated that way. Here's what I said that day on our "Plugged in Extra" segment:

*My longevity is a reflection of what Fox 8 is all about. We're Cleveland's Own and I'm from Cleveland, I grew up in Glenville, went to Shaw High School. I went to Tri-C, then Kent. I never left here, and I started working here at [Channel 8] as soon as I graduated. Virgil Dominic was the one who hired me, and it was Mike Renda who put me on the Morning Show, and Paul Perozeni and Andy Fishman, Mark Singer... Margaret Daykin, Darren Sweeney–I'm blessed with all these people. Me and Sissy go back a long way, God bless you.*

*Like I said before, this is the one station in town where we believe in stability... we are family. Sometimes we argue, fight and fuss, but we're family and that's just the bottom line. I'm so very blessed to be here and so humbled...a kid from the eastside of Cleveland and East Cleveland, I would've never thought that I would be here for 40 years.*

*It's nothing but a blessing and I'm grateful and thankful, once again I love you guys and our viewers. Bless you for putting up with me for 40 years. It's been something and hopefully, it'll continue, and I appreciate you so much.*

*It's been so many stories over the years, man. Herb Thomas, he was my guy and he passed away about a year ago and I miss him tremendously. It's been a great run, it really has.*

*It's been a blessing and let's keep being number one guys!*

**I meant every word.**

# Chapter 28

# Scrapbook

My beloved Mom in her young days.

My dad in the 1980s.

1960s with my cousins.
That's me wearing
the glasses.

Mom, me, and my aunts
Martha and Florence.

My beautiful wife LaVerne.

On a date with my lovely wife, LaVerne.

**Big family at Christmas.**

With Laverne, Danielle, and Tyshin.

With my brother, Judge William Dawson in his courtroom.

With my queen and we both looking clean!

**Interviewing author/speaker Deante Young
during his book launch event.**

**Covering a breaking news event in
Orlando, Florida while on vacation!**

Suited up and
looking clean.

I like to make a statement
with my fashion.

Another picture of my grandchildren.
Don't they look like I spoil them?

**Me with my oldest daughter Tammy.**

**My son Tyshin and me.**

At the 2015 Wooly Bear Festival with the legend himself, Dick Goddard.

With Stefani Schaefer and Kristi Capel at the Republican National Convention.

Celebrating and covering the parade for the Cleveland Cavaliers' 2016 NBA championship with Sissy.

Watching a Cavs game with my son, Tyshin.

Christmas morning with the grandkids in 2018.

Family time with my children a long time ago!

Daddy's girls: My daughter Crystal in blue (left) and Tammy in red (right).

My son Tyshin and me in the field.
He's a natural!

With my youngest daughter,
Danielle on Father's Day 2016.

**Reporting live from the White House
following the 2016 Presidential election.**

**Just chillin' with my daughter Crystal.**

Rocking the afro back in my young and cool days!

Senior year at Shaw High School. Look at those sideburns!

The "Wayne Dawson Celebrity Bowl-a-Thon" in 2019.

The Dawson Foundation
coat giveaway.

**Me and my dear friend, the great Herb Thomas.**

Behind the scenes view of me, Kristi Capel (left)
and Sissy during a commercial break.

A surprise appearance from my wonderful family during the 40th
anniversary celebration at Fox 8 studios, which was broadcast live.

**Celebrating Grace Tabernacle's 35th anniversary with my beautiful wife LaVerne, and my spiritual mentor, guest speaker, Rev. Dr. Stephen Rowan.**

**With the lovely Natalie Herbick on the set of her show,**
***New Day Cleveland.***

**With the one and only Richard "Zoom" Scott**
**after church service at Grace.**

# Chapter 29

# Deante's Closing Thoughts

It's been a whirlwind experience getting to know Wayne Dawson and his family. More than anything else, it's been a privilege and an honor to speak with, learn from, and laugh with everyone that's closest to him. Trying to condense someone's life into a book is a challenging endeavor, but it's practically impossible to convey the true scope of anyone's journey in even a thousand pages.

Wayne has managed to outshine his own glowing reputation simply by being a beacon of positivity, humility, selflessness and humanity IN REAL LIFE. When I first approached him in November 2021 with the idea of doing his memoirs, I was shocked that there had never been a book written about him at all.

He never accepts the term "legend" whenever I refer to him as such, but no matter how someone chooses to view Dawson's life, it deserved to be written about many years ago.

And yes, he *is* legendary.

His journey has been theatrical in many ways; the relentlessly self-confident black kid who came of age in the early 1970s and viewed on-screen pimps as role models.

The adolescent that went from straight A's in elementary school to needing summer school and night school to *barely* graduate high school.

The weed smoking, alcohol drinking teenager whose father abandoned the family leading Wayne to soon become a dedicated young father to his own child.

The hyper focused young man who got through college on food stamps and financial aid only to achieve outlier success as a television broadcaster and in-demand speaker.

The once insatiable womanizer became a committed husband and sold out for God as the pastor of a church. His triumph is *our* triumph because he empowers everyone with his own jaw-dropping journey that's illustrated in these pages.

Wayne Dawson has proven with his own trials and tribulations that grit, determination, self-belief, patience, evolution and an uncompromising belief in God are the hallmarks of success.

They are in fact, *the seeds of greatness.*

It has been an endlessly wonderful blessing and honor to collaborate with Wayne Dawson on this essential and historic project. His legacy is still being written, but his far-reaching impact is etched in stone.

Just ask anyone that's ever met this great man of God.

-D.Y.

# Chapter 30

# Wayne's Closing Thoughts

As I look back on my life while dictating my memoir to Deante Young in "The Seeds of Greatness Are Within You," I am humbled at how the Lord has used me, the least among us, to make a difference in the lives of others.

My life has been full of ups and downs and turnarounds and has been far less than perfect, but the Lord has used me even with all of my imperfections and shortcomings. This is my message to the reader: no matter who you are, where you come from or where you are right now, the seeds of greatness are within you, because the Creator has given you everything you need to be great, but it takes hard work, focus, determination and the ability to learn from your defeats and setbacks. I've always looked at obstacles as stepping stones on the road to greater achievement. My prayer is that something in my story, be it good or bad, will inspire you to be the best you can be.

My journey has been a blessed one, staying at one television station for more than 40 years in an industry that's often turbulent and always changing, being licensed and ordained into the ministry, and eventually being called to pastor. It's all been a glorious ride. I am so thankful to those who've helped me along the way.

I also want to thank the viewers who've watched me down through the years and the Fox 8 management who have always been very supportive.

Also, a special shout-out to my main man Dr. John Walker Jr. He's a retired pastor now living in Sarasota, Florida who's served as a trusted confidant and friend throughout the years.

I want to thank Deante Young for the time and effort he put into making my memoir a reality.

Finally, thank you for reading my memoir, and hopefully it has blessed you in some way. Everyone has a story. Everyone is creating a legacy, so my challenge to you is to autograph everything you do with your best effort because, "The Seeds of Greatness Are Within You."

Wayne

# Acknowledgments

This book has been a labor of love and a blessing from my Heavenly Father. The list of people I want to acknowledge is much longer than I can wrap my mind around, but I'll try.

My Lord and Savior, Jesus Christ is at the top of the list followed by my beautiful wife and partner in the ministry LaVerne, my beloved mother, Annie, my father, George, my wonderful children, Tammy, Crystal, Tyshin and Danielle, my loving cousin Melva and Sharon, the mother of my two oldest daughters, all of whom have also been very instrumental in my life.

I also want to acknowledge the future of our family: my grandchildren Karina, Makenna, Trace, Kyle, Kaleb, Moriah, Saphera and Brooklynn, along with my niece and nephew Aria and William Jr. Special recognition goes to my brother, Judge William and his wife Elsie for our work together with the Dawson Foundation.

43 years broadcasting at one television station is nearly two-thirds of my life, and I'd like to thank my Fox 8 family for all of their support. The list is not comprehensive, but I'd like to acknowledge my current and past co-workers on the morning show: Stefani Schaefer, Kristi Capel, Todd Meany, Scott Sabol, Richard "Zoom" Scott, Kenny Crumpton, Natalie Herbick Alexis Walters, Jessica Dill, Stacey Frey, Patty Harken, Jenn Harcher, Alexis Walters, Tracy McCool and Andre Bernier.

In my years at Channel 8, I've been blessed with wonderful and encouraging management including Paul Perozeni, Andy Fishman, Mike Renda, Virgil Dominic, Greg Easterly, Mark Singer, Darren Sweeney, and longtime friend Margaret Daykin.

I'd also like to shout out my entire Grace Tabernacle Baptist Church family with special honor going to our First Lady Emeritus Juliet Pryce, along with my spiritual mentors Reverend Dr. Stephen Rowan, Bishop Joey Johnson, Pastor Kevin James, Rev. Dr. David Hunter and last but not least, my best friend and confidant Dr. John Walker, Jr.

In closing, I'd also like to recognize my life long high school friends James Wesley, Marvin Freeman and Romero Moreno.

Finally, to my Phi Beta Sigma brothers… GOMOB!

# About the Authors

WAYNE DAWSON joined Cleveland's WJKW-TV (now WJW) Channel 8 in 1979 after a successful college career at Kent State University. He began as a reporter with the news station and became a full-timer in 1982, the same year he pledged with the Phi Beta Sigma fraternity. For the past 30 years, Dawson has been an anchorman with what is now Fox 8 News in Cleveland. He's been the lead anchor on *Fox 8 News in the Morning* since 1999.

Dawson, a native Clevelander born in the Glenville section, covered many notable news stories and events for decades including the first HBCU college football game held in Cleveland, the Republican National Convention, the Million Man March, the first anniversary of when Dr. Martin Luther King Jr.'s birthday became a national holiday and more.

He's a tireless public speaker and has interviewed many high-profile individuals such as President George H.W. Bush, LeBron James, and Snoop Dogg. He has received numerous awards and commendations highlighted by his inductions into the Broadcasters Hall of Fame, the Cleveland Press Club, and the NATAS Silver Circle.

Dawson is also an 11-time Emmy winner, a recipient of the Chuck Heaton award for social service, and is the co-founder of the Dawson Foundation, a charitable endeavor that awards scholarships to deserving students as well as giveaways to less fortunate individuals.

Wayne is currently in his 43rd year at Channel 8 and has been the pastor at Grace Tabernacle Baptist Church in Lyndhurst, Ohio since 2018. He is the proud father of four wonderful children and eight amazing grandchildren.

For the past 25 years, Wayne had been married to his lovely wife, LaVerne who is also the First Lady at Grace.

DEANTE YOUNG is a native Clevelander (Glenville) and is the founder and Chief Creative Architect of Dirty Truth Publishing, LLC as well as its head author. He is also a speaker and specializes in writing and speaking about personal development, life lessons and self-doubt.

He is the author of seven nonfiction books since 2021 and has a library of content on those topics at Medium.com.

Young also covers those subjects as well as overcoming limiting beliefs on his podcast and is the executive producer and host of the new digital series, "Deante Speaks to Cleveland."

He is the proud father of two amazing daughters and is based in Greater Cleveland, Ohio.

Deante's books and apparel are available at DirtyTruthPublishing.com and his books are also available at Amazon, Cuyahoga County libraries and other online and local retailers.

All photographs contained in the "Scrapbook" chapter are courtesy of Wayne Dawson's personal collection, and a few are from Deante Young's personal collection.